Barron's Dog Training Bible

by Andrea Arden
Photos by Seth Casteel

Dedication

For my father, George J. Arden, Sr. I am grateful that his love of animals was contagious and that each dog that comes into my life is a happy reminder of him.

Acknowledgments

Enormous thanks to all those who have so generously shared their knowledge. Thank you for providing me with greater insight into the hearts and minds of dogs.

To Angela Tartaro: Your editorial efforts went above and beyond what any author could hope for. Working with you was an absolute pleasure.

Special thanks to JoAnne Basinger, Katrina Krings, Mike Lustig, and Dan Tambourine, and to the staff and volunteers at Animal Haven Shelter for your hard work and dedication and for allowing me to play a part in your efforts to help cats and dogs in need.

Thanks to my brother George, sister-in-law Yvonne, and my nephews, George III, Ulysses, Lynden, and Harrison. I couldn't ask for a more wonderful family.

About the Author

Andrea Arden can be seen on Animal Planet's *Underdog to Wonderdog*, *Dogs101*, and *Cats101*. She was the trainer for *The Pet Department*, FX's Emmy award-winning daily show, and appears regularly on *The Today Show*. Her appearances also include *20/20*, *Dateline NBC*, *Queer Eye for the Straight Guy*, *Live with Regis & Kelly*, *The View*, *CBS News*, *CNN*, *Fox*, *PBS*, *Fox News*, and *Lifetime*, as well as numerous radio shows.

Andrea is the director of Andrea Arden Dog Training and was named the best dog trainer in New York by the *Daily News* and *New York*, *W*, *Time Out*, and *Quest* magazines. She has served on the Board of Directors of the Association of Pet Dog Trainers (APDT) and currently serves on the Board of Directors of Animal Haven Shelter. She is a Certified Pet Dog Trainer, a Certified Pet Partners Team evaluator for the Delta Society, and a certified evaluator for the AKC's Canine Good Citizen (CGC) test.

Andrea is the author of five training books, was the behavior columnist for *Dog Fancy* and *The New York Dog* magazines, and is a contributing writer for the *AKC Gazette*, *Modern Dog*, and numerous other publications. You can visit Andrea's website at *www.andreaarden.com*.

All information and advice contained in this book has been reviewed by a veterinarian.

A Word About Pronouns

Many dog lovers feel that the pronoun "it" is not appropriate when referring to a pet that can be such a wonderful part of our lives. For this reason, dogs are described as "he" throughout this book unless the topic specifically relates to female dogs. This by no means infers any preference, nor should it be taken as an indication that either sex is problematic.

Photos © Seth Casteel
www.LittleFriendsPhoto.com

All inquiries should be addressed to:
Barron's Educational Series, Inc.
250 Wireless Boulevard
Hauppauge, New York 11788
www.barronseduc.com

ISBN: 978-0-7641-6433-0

Library of Congress Catalog Card No: 2011012153

Library of Congress Cataloging-in-Publication
Arden, Andrea.
   Barron's dog training bible / by Andrea Arden.
   p. cm.
   Includes bibliographical references and index.
   ISBN 978-0-7641-6433-0 (alk. paper)
   1. Dogs--Training. I. Title. II. Title: Dog training bible.
   SF431.A744 2011
   636.7'0835--dc22   2011012153

Printed in China

9 8 7 6 5 4 3 2 1

CONTENTS

CONTENTS

CONTENTS

PREFACE

As any pet parent will tell you, the sheer breadth of information available about teaching dogs can be overwhelming, contradictory, and therefore, utterly confusing. Trust your own instincts regarding the logic of any advice. Consider the potential side effects, both positive and negative, and how you suspect a specific approach might affect your dog and his relationship with you.

At the core, the process of teaching your dog should be about great friends sharing time together in an effort to facilitate better communication and understanding of one another. Being a good canine parent requires some education. Sometimes just a little will do, and sometimes people need what amounts to a Ph.D. in Dogology. Whichever the case, this book ensures you are on the right path—one where you can obtain the knowledge required to teach your canine companion in the easiest, most effective, and most enjoyable way possible.

This is not a book that needs to be read cover to cover. By all means, turn first to the pages that best apply to you. However, whether you are teaching basic manners or aiming to resolve behavior problems, have a puppy or senior dog, I also hope that you read the material that may not at first seem to be relevant to you and your dog. The behavior of resource guarding, for example, may never be an issue with your dog. But, every pet parent should know what it is and what signs to look for so they know if trouble is brewing on the horizon.

Perhaps most importantly, the next time your dog looks longingly into your eyes, consider that he is trying his best to understand you and what you want. The goal of this book is to equip you with the knowledge to respond to your dog with a better understanding of his unique perspective, needs, and motivations.

Take great pride that you have endeavored to learn more about the heart and mind of your dog. He will surely thank you with a bond and friendship like no other.

Andrea Arden

The Fido Factor: Raising a Companion Dog in the 21st Century

The evolution of the relationship between people and dogs is a commentary on our existence, our evolution, and our desire for companionship and unconditional love. Dogs can improve the quality and duration of our lives, and they have surely earned the title of man *and* woman's best friend.

The simple daily pleasures that dogs bring to our lives consistently confirms their role as helpful, tolerant, and forgiving companions. Canine loyalty and affection often surpasses our expectations of our best human friends. There is no doubt that life is never the same once you have welcomed a dog into your heart and home.

Yet, for all the ways dogs positively influence our lives, this inter-species relationship can also pose unexpected complications. The challenges of raising a well-mannered, sociable canine companion can lead to frustration, guilt, and disappointment. But that doesn't have to be the case. With a solid understanding of canine needs, these feelings are easily replaced with patience, realistic expectations, and the satisfaction that comes from accomplishing goals with your dog. You can provide your dog with the skills to become trusting and compliant. This will result in one of the most rewarding relationships you could hope for.

The Evolution of the Canine-Human Bond

In the beginning, dogs most likely chose to be close to people because this proximity provided opportunities to scavenge leftovers. Therefore, in some ways this became a process of self-domestication. People wisely recognized the benefits of accepting canine companionship in their lives. Dogs aided man's struggle for survival, and they were ultimately employed for many purposes, including guarding, hunting, hauling, and providing warmth. Like humans, most dogs were required to multi-task, and as such, they became invaluable members of what could be deemed a mutual admiration society.

The enduring friendship between dogs and people is based largely on the fact that both are highly social creatures. Dogs understand that it is

much easier to survive as a member of a group rather than on their own. In the wild, these relationships are formed with members of their own species, known as packs. Through the process of domestication, dogs also learned to form cooperative relationships with other species, and they were superbly suited to aid people in countless ways. At this point, it might be more accurate to say they have become members of our families.

Selective Breeding

As this mutually beneficial relationship progressed, people began to prize dogs for specific qualities. Some were valued for their alertness, while others were valued for speed, or responsiveness to learning. This was the beginning of selective breeding for desired traits. It has resulted in hundreds of breeds that encompass a vast array of distinct characteristics. In every breed, certain traits are accentuated to improve their ability to assist us, and in some cases simply to be beautiful, enjoyable companions. For instance, the sighthounds were bred for extreme speed and keen

TRAINING TRUTH

Focus on Companion Dogs

People certainly valued canine companionship during the early stages of the canine-human bond. But at that point in time, no one had the resources to keep dogs solely as friends. People were far more concerned with the contribution that dogs could make toward everyone's survival. As a result, they became more specialized for particular jobs. We have spent thousands of years accentuating, appreciating, and benefiting from every breed's unique working function.

Our world has changed, and our reliance on dogs as working companions has decreased. There are still plenty of dogs with day jobs such as bomb, drug, and cancer-sniffing dogs, as well as police and service dogs—to name just a few. However, the focus of our relationships with our dogs has shifted from work to companionship. Regardless of their original function, most dogs now live their lives as our companions. Some breeds adapt to this modern role more easily than others. In some cases, it is at odds with the breed's underlying behavioral traits.

eyesight, to hunt fast game over the flat open terrain of the Middle East. On the other side of Asia, the Pekingese was developed in China's Imperial Court to resemble a lion, guard the palace, and act as a loyal, dignified companion to the royal family.

Every Dog Needs a Job

All dogs need a job, regardless of their size, type, ancestry, or age. The goal in creating a job description for today's pet dogs is to provide them with an outlet for their physical and mental energy. The easiest way to do this is by teaching skills that will become your dog's job. Dogs that are occupied with doing the things we want have little time or energy for activities

TRAINER'S TIP

Although dogs want to be accepted into our social groups, they don't automatically understand the rules. They require our thoughtful guidance and an understanding of their needs as they learn to recognize and choose appropriate behaviors. Family members should discuss this and agree on an approach to training and a set of clearly defined goals for future reference.

we don't want them to do. As a result, the underlying canine and human relationship is enhanced.

Training not only enhances your dog's well-being, it's also an important social responsibility. Whether it's fair or not, a dog's conduct is viewed as a reflection of his family and their ability to be responsible owners.

Teaching our dogs to be well-mannered should not be seen as a desire to exert our will over them. It is vital to their safety and ensures that they will be warmly welcomed in their community and in our homes.

Setting Realistic Expectations

Dogs that remain in one loving and responsible home throughout their lives generally have two things in common; their families have realistic expectations and a commitment to ongoing education. When setting expectations, consider your dog's age, temperament, activity level, and health.

It's equally important to honestly assess your ability to follow through with teaching your dog to do what you want on a consistent basis. An honest assessment of these variable factors will prevent frustration and encourage success. Generally, dogs only fail when asked to do things for which they aren't prepared. This happens when your efforts to teach them something are inconsistent, or when they are not yet mentally or physically equipped to learn the concept.

Commitment and Compliance

Most people start out with the best of intentions when they get a dog. They imagine how their dog will behave (for example, he won't jump onto the furniture). Yet, in a short time, their dog behavior wish list has been replaced by a list of behavior problems and excuses for why they developed.

Inconsistency is a major reason for this. Good intentions are meaningless without realistic expectations and a consistent agenda of helping your dog

CHECKLIST

Training Expectations

Most people share the same general training goals. They hope for a dog that is friendly and safe, mannerly, responsive to requests, housetrained, and trustworthy when unsupervised. However, specific expectations vary. Clarify your goals by making a list of behaviors you consider important in your dog. For example:

Dog Behavior Wish List

- How would you like your dog to greet people?
- Where should your dog eliminate?
- What should he chew, and more importantly, refrain from chewing?
- How should he behave when left alone?
- When is barking permissible and when should it stop?
- What cues or commands should he respond to reliably?
- How should he react when you take something away from him?
- Is he allowed to jump on the furniture?

While your family is setting goals and expectations for your dog's behavior, you should also discuss the reasons why they are important. This way, everyone will be motivated to follow through with training. For instance, a dog that doesn't *come when called* can be seriously hurt if he happens to slip from his leash on a busy street. A dog that consistently eliminates on rugs is in danger of being relinquished to a shelter. Consistently encouraging your dog's behavior in the right direction requires a team effort.

Curb Your Frustration

Dogs thrive in situations where rules and boundaries are clearly defined and communicated to them in a calm, consistent manner.

Most families consider their expectations of dog behavior to be simple. Therefore, it should be easy for their dog to understand and follow these rules. Although dogs are adept at integrating themselves into our homes and hearts, the human world is a complicated place. Behaviors that are perfectly normal and acceptable in the canine world, such as marking, barking, digging, scavenging, humping, and threatening in the face of fear, are often at odds with human expectations.

It is unfair and unrealistic to assume that your dog will automatically understand what is expected of him. You must make a consistent effort to communicate this information if you want your dog to make the right behavior choices. In many cases, well intentioned, loving pet parents may treat their dogs unfairly because they are frustrated by their dog's misbehavior. As a result, the dog becomes overwhelmed and confused.

A great deal of frustration can be avoided if you learn to recognize your dog's propensity to behave in certain ways. This may be due to genetics and/or experiences. You should certainly seek to improve your dog's behavior, but some dogs may always need special assistance when facing particular challenges. This can include dogs that have social issues in the presence of people or other dogs, and dogs with resource-guarding issues (guarding things they consider valuable, such as chew toys and food bowls).

In these cases, training should focus on managing the dog's time to minimize situations that may exacerbate the problem in addition to creating more positive responses.

learn the behaviors that you want from him. You cannot expect your dog to be mannerly and quiet if you are in the habit of praising him for jumping around and howling with excitement when you arrive home. This lack of consistency can be quite confusing for dogs and will most likely lead to disappointment for the family in regard to their dog's overall behavior.

Time to Teach

Once you have set realistic goals and made a commitment to teach your dog, it is time to decide the all-important question of how to achieve your goals. The effort required for this can vary greatly depending on your lifestyle and training skills, as well as the dog's age, genetics, and past experiences. Some dogs require more structure and repetition than others. Your goals and training pace must match your dog's strengths and limitations.

Considering all of this potential for variability, one might expect that vastly different approaches are warranted when teaching individual dogs. Regardless of the dog's age, breed, or lineage, or the family's expectations and experience, the overall approach to training is basically the same. This applies to teaching new behaviors and modifying existing ones.

PAWS TO CONSIDER

Regardless of your training goals or your dog's unique temperament, the training process must be built on a foundation of trust. This is the basis of efficient, effective training, and a healthy and happy relationship with your dog.

Trust as the Foundation for Teaching

A trusting relationship is central to the training process. It is the support net for your dog as he learns to cope with the experiences and circumstances of the human world and what is expected of him.

Training facilitates communication and strengthens your bond with your dog. However, the dog must believe that his people are trustworthy before this can happen. Your dog won't feel motivated to pay attention to your directions unless he values your guidance and wants to understand what you have to say.

This is why consideration of the long-range impact of a particular method is so important when choosing a training approach for your dog. A dog's responsiveness to learning is motivated by his desire to be

Coercive Training

Something can be dangerous to your dog without being physically harmful—it can be psychologically detrimental. In fact, many of the problems dogs have are emotionally based as opposed to physically based.

Choosing an aversive approach that causes your dog mental or physical pain should be avoided at all costs. The negative side effects of a punishment- and coercion-based approach are many, and they include even more serious behavior problems related to aggression, fear, and anxiety. Even if your dog doesn't end up with these problems, it is not in his best interest or in yours, nor does it bode well for creating an enthusiastically compliant canine companion.

part of a social group and his willingness to trust his people. Trust fosters cooperation, and a cooperative dog is easily guided toward appropriate behavior (i.e., their job) in any given situation.

Some might presume that a fun, loving relationship with a dog is contradictory to training. This is probably based on the misleading idea that training is primarily about discipline and correction. In fact, teaching your dog what is expected of him in a calm, gentle, and gradual manner is the most effective and efficient route to success.

Leader, Guide, Teacher, or Coach?

For the past 25 years or so, there has been a lot of talk in the dog world about being your dog's leader. Some feel this aptly describes the role we should take with our dogs. Others feel that this word implies a military approach to the canine-human relationship and a need for punitive training techniques.

However, we expect dogs to survive and thrive in a world that is quite foreign to them. Therefore, it seems logical that they would best adjust with a person (or a family) to lead them in the right direction.

Human language is vastly different from the way dogs communicate and our rules are often at odds with normal—and in some cases instinctual—dog behavior (for example, don't dig, bark, chew, jump up to greet, chase, hump, or eliminate wherever you like). Dogs are not equipped to navigate our world on their own, and leading them through these oftentimes trying experiences should be our goal. A mentally and behaviorally healthy canine companion is a happy follower.

If the word leader is at odds with your sensibilities, you may feel more comfortable referring to yourself as your pup's guide, coach, or even teacher. Regardless of the word used to describe this position, the job comes down to helping your pup earn a graduate degree as a mannerly, social canine in the human world. So, what does this job description entail? First and foremost, you must formulate a game plan or a curriculum to achieve your training goals (see "Setting Realistic Expectations" on page 4).

Picking a Positive Approach

Once you have a concrete plan, it is time to decide the all-important question of how to help your dog learn the fundamentals of canine etiquette. The formula for a mentally and behaviorally healthy canine companion begins with teaching him through positive motivation. This sets the foundation for your dog's good manners, whether you are together at home, going for a walk, participating in a dog sport such as agility or flyball, or leaving him alone while you are out. It is one of the kindest things you can do for your dog, and the surest way to build a lifelong, trusting, and cooperative friendship. Choosing a thoughtful, positive approach to teaching your canine companion ensures that he will achieve his graduate degree as a well-mannered dog.

Understanding Your Dog

D ogs work very hard to understand us, and they deserve the same consideration in return. Dogs and humans perceive social interaction as both necessary and desirable, but we express ourselves in distinctly different ways. Failing to understand your dog's motivations, drives, social signals, and developmental phases can lead to miscommunication and confusion. In order to elicit and strengthen desirable canine behaviors you must learn to effectively communicate with your dog.

A Wolf Inside?

At one time, it was believed that studying the social behavior of wolves would provide insights into dog behavior. There are similarities between dogs and wolves, and wolf behavior can provide some insights into dog behavior. However, there are also vast differences. Observing the behavior of a group of wild animals cannot provide realistic information about coexisting with a domestic species in your home. This idea is overly simplistic and sometimes detrimental.

It was also discovered that many theories about wolf pack structure were inaccurate. Wolf packs are cooperative and complex social structures. Their behavior is designed to ensure the mutual survival of the group. Body language is used to maintain harmony and minimize confrontations. Actual fighting is rare, and active (voluntary) submission is far more common than forced submission, especially for puppies.

Unfortunately, misconceptions about the role of dominance and aggression in wolf packs have become ingrained in popular culture. It has been used to rationalize the use of punishment during training because people continue to accept the idea that properly disciplining a dog like an alpha wolf is the way to gain and maintain dominant status.

Setting and enforcing reasonable rules and boundaries is a far more effective and humane way to become your dog's leader. Rather than intimidating him with brute force, help him follow the rules by controlling his resources. This way he learns to perceive his family as a support system. Adhering to

DANGER!

Training strategies based on the notion of attaining dominance over a dog range from dangerous to pointless. Maintaining control over a dog through intimidation and bullying is unjustified and likely to intensify behavior problems stemming from fear and aggression. Some dogs respond to this approach with justified confusion, mistrust, and fear. In order to protect themselves from further abuse, they may retaliate with any and all weapons at their disposal—including their teeth. Use your brain rather than inflicting pain to lead your dog.

his family's expectations becomes his way to ensure his acceptance within his family and access to what he wants.

Dominance and Submission

Dominance and submission are two terms that are widely misunderstood, oversimplified, and overused. For example, a host of canine behavior problems are misdiagnosed as attempts to exert dominance. In fact, individual dogs often display both dominant and submissive behavior, shifting from one to the other according to their environment. A dog's status is regularly influenced by the presence of other animals and people, as well as other environmental factors. For example, an adult dog in a room full of puppies would most likely be dominant over the younger and less experienced dogs and would thereby have greater access to resources. Surrounded by other adult dogs in a park, this dog may behave more submissively in order to get along with the others.

In all areas of life, dogs do what works for them. A dog who mounts his owner might be labeled as "dominant," but what does that mean? It has become a catchphrase to pigeonhole behaviors rather than examining them. In truth, a dog that mounts his owner might be displaying aggression, playing, or simply seeking attention. Deciphering the motivation for a particular behavior is difficult. Labeling a dog as dominant eliminates the need to analyze the problem. Even worse, the "solution" for a dog labeled as dominant often involves punishment and force, which often intensifies the problem. Depending on your definition, a dominant or confident dog is not necessarily a problem dog. In fact, a less confident dog who is attempting to raise his status can be more troublesome because he will habitually test and challenge boundaries.

Indications of Dominant Behavior

A dog's posture usually becomes more rigid if he intends to threaten. Typical signs of dominance displays include standing tall, with tail and ears at attention. A dominant dog might also mount another dog or place his head or paws over the other dog's body. The combination of adrenaline and heightened arousal also causes hackles (hair on the back of neck and back) to be raised.

Raised hackles may be intended to signify a threat. But, physiologically this is an uncontrollable or unconscious reaction that must be interpreted in context. Both neutered and unneutered males and females engage in this behavior with both sexes. Likewise, mounting behavior is context specific. In some cases, it has a reproductive function. But, it also occurs during play and does not necessarily indicate that a dog is trying to reproduce or assert dominance.

Indications of Submissive Behavior

A submissive dog uses his body to express his desire to avoid aggression and intention to do no harm. His ears and tail are lowered, and his gaze is averted. He crouches, turns away, or rolls on his back.

"Good Dog Myth"

Otherwise known as the "Lassie syndrome," the "good dog myth" refers to the notion that dogs are innately motivated to please us and make us happy. Dogs that seem to have this propensity are considered "good dogs," and those that don't are labeled as "bad dogs." Needless to say, many dogs fail to live up to these unrealistic expectations. Many people hope for a dog that is solely devoted to pleasing them. Unfortunately, this concept completely disregards the laws of nature. A survival instinct motivates most animal behavior, not the desire to please other animals. Most canine behavior is motivated by the desire to gain access to important resources like food, attention, and comfortable resting spots. The basic canine philosophy asks: What is in it for me right now? What is rewarding? What is safe? What is not? They can be manipulative and self-centered when trying to gain access to these resources, which is okay.

Well-mannered dogs *do* want to please people, but this is not motivated by an innate, altruistic drive. Through training, they learn that doing as we ask will increase their access to the things they find rewarding.

A Dog's Eye View: Scents and Sensibility

Dogs and humans share the same major senses, but the scope of information gleaned through these senses is quite different. Your dog's senses greatly influence his behavior, motivations, and responsiveness to your guidance. They can lead him to be distracted from the task at hand and can also be used to reinforce desired behavior. For example, you can reward your dog for walking nicely by your side by stopping and allowing him to enjoy an interesting scent he may encounter. Alternatively, you can let him pull you toward this enticing sidewalk scent, thus rewarding him for dragging you along for the ride.

Smell

This is where dogs truly shine. Dogs are far more attuned to and affected by smells than we are. They receive a vast amount of information by air scenting and sniffing the ground. It is believed that the area of the dog's brain devoted to analyzing smells is approximately forty times larger than the same region in the human brain. The dog's sense of smell opens up a vast realm of olfactory experience and can seem to dominate their brain and their behavior.

BETTER BEHAVIOR

The word "manipulative" has serious negative connotations. But, it need not imply a malicious intent. We habitually attempt to influence canine behavior, and dogs attempt to do the same with us. There is nothing wrong with this approach as long as it's done fairly and responsibly. For instance, we use this approach to guide specific canine behaviors in a direction that we consider appropriate. For example, a dog may bark to gain attention or elicit a specific response from his owner, such as fixing his dinner. Essentially, the dog is trying to manipulate human behavior through barking. Alternatively, we can teach the dog to sit rather than bark to elicit the response of dinner service from his owner. In both situations, neither party is acting in a negative way; each party is simply negotiating social mores in order to get what he or she wants.

It is impossible to truly understand the importance of scent for dogs and how this sense affects their behavior. Humans have used the canine sense of smell to their advantage in hunting, search-and-rescue work, and bomb and drug detection. Dogs have been trained to detect everything from cancer cells to bed bugs, and they deserve our gratitude for the many ways we have benefited from their scenting abilities. They also deserve our consideration for the amount of information they process via this sense, and the fact that they can be distracted by things we can't perceive. Rather than being frustrated, consider how to best motivate your dog to pay attention in a distracting environment.

Sight

Dogs also see differently than we do because their sense of sight is tailored for hunting. They have superior motion sensitivity and can detect slight changes in the environment at great distances. This is why they easily react to a small, fast moving object such as a ball or rabbit. On the other hand, they have less ability to discern details of stationary objects. For instance, your dog may not easily detect you if you stand still 500 yards away. But, the

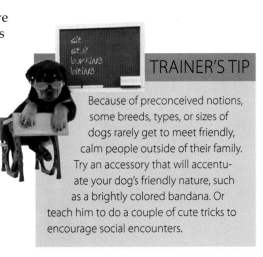

TRAINER'S TIP

Because of preconceived notions, some breeds, types, or sizes of dogs rarely get to meet friendly, calm people outside of their family. Try an accessory that will accentuate your dog's friendly nature, such as a brightly colored bandana. Or teach him to do a couple of cute tricks to encourage social encounters.

15

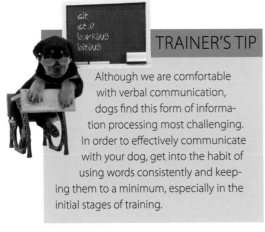

TRAINER'S TIP

Although we are comfortable with verbal communication, dogs find this form of information processing most challenging. In order to effectively communicate with your dog, get into the habit of using words consistently and keeping them to a minimum, especially in the initial stages of training.

moment you begin to move, he will recognize you.

Dogs have superior night vision, and need only about one-fourth of the light we do to see in the dark. They also generally have better peripheral vision, but less ability to differentiate colors. A dog's ability to perceive colors is the equivalent of a red/green color-blindness. They see green, yellow, and orange as yellowish, and blue-greens as grey.

Hearing

Dogs can detect sounds far higher on the auditory spectrum, from far greater distances. This explains why they react to things we cannot hear.

Dogs often tilt their heads in order to better locate the source of a sound, and their ear mobility allows them to maneuver their ears to precisely pinpoint the location of sounds. However, this ability varies. For example, a Bloodhound's long, low-set ears have less maneuverability. Instead, they rely on their keen sense of smell. In contrast, the ears of an Alaskan Malamute are high set and highly mobile.

Taste

In this particular sense, we exceed canine abilities with our 9,000 taste buds compared with their 1,700. The dog's sense of taste takes a back seat to other senses. However, smell plays a huge part in this sensory experience. For instance, a head cold and stuffy nose compromises your ability to taste food. Dogs rely more on their olfactory sense than their taste buds to evaluate the palatability of food.

Touch

Touch plays a vital role in the social structure of a dog's life, beginning with a puppy's interactions with his mother and littermates. Dogs touch for warmth and to solicit food, initiate greetings, maintain social bonding, and engage in some confrontational interactions. They may nuzzle, mouth, nibble, paw, bump, push, or lie next to another dog. The broad actions of touch are similar when used for both friendly and unfriendly interactions. It is the degree, intensity, and contact that defines its meaning. For example, a dog may mouth, paw, and mount his best canine friend in good fun. He might also do this with a confrontational intent.

As social creatures, we share our dogs' need for physical contact. However, dogs, like people, vary in their response to proximity and touch. We must be aware of how they perceive certain forms of touch. A dog's reaction depends on many factors, including his sensitivity and mood, as well as who is touching him. Consider which areas of your dog's body

are most sensitive (usually paws and muzzle) and which areas he enjoys having touched. Scratching his ear or rubbing his tummy can be used to reinforce desirable behaviors. A pat that one dog considers enjoyable might seem intimidating to another. Restricting or restraining your dog for a prolonged period is likely to be perceived differently than gentle pressure.

A dog's aversion to touch can be an underlying cause of behavior issues, such as aggression. Dogs can and should be taught to enjoy human touch for bonding and safety, and so that it can be used as a reward.

PAWS TO CONSIDER

Proximity

Dogs typically approach and remain close to people or other animals when they feel comfortable in their presence, but there are exceptions to this rule. A dog may, on occasion, approach in order to intimidate or test the other animal's reaction to his presence.

Canine Communication

Developing a better understanding of "dog speak" opens the lines of communication by helping to prevent misunderstandings due to misinterpretation.

Dogs communicate through body language, vocalization, and scents. Each indicator can provide clues about your dogs feelings. But, they are not absolutes. For example, a wagging tail does not always indicate a happy, relaxed state of mind. Typical canine gestures can have different meanings when directed toward dogs or people. If your dog rests his head on your lap, he is indicating a desire for attention and comfort. He may be indicating something quite different when he rests his head across another dog's shoulders.

Each canine communication signal can have multiple meanings, and dogs generally combine them when signaling their thoughts and intentions. You must pay attention to all body parts, frequency, tone, overall body language, and context to accurately understand what your dog is saying.

Some people are more precise and articulate, and some dogs are better equipped to interpret and use some signals. This can be due to genetics, experience, or physiology. At first glance, Nordic breeds like Siberian Huskies and Pomeranians may seem threatening simply because they normally carry their ears and tails high, and their coats stand off the body. A dog with poor social skills may erroneously conclude that these physical features signal a dominance display, just as we can jump to conclusions based on someone's appearance. Muscular breeds like Bulldogs generally have a stiffer body posture, and physical tension is a normal aspect of their physical demeanor rather than an indicator of an aroused mental state. On the other hand, a rangy Bloodhound may appear calm and relaxed when he is highly aroused.

Dogs also vary in their ability to interpret body language. For example, some dogs quickly back off when approaching another dog whose body language communicates fear or discomfort. Socially awkward or immature dogs may ignore these signals. They will approach, offer a greeting, or try to engage in play even though the other dog is clearly not interested.

Calming Signals and Body Language

Dogs generally prefer to resolve disagreements without engaging in direct conflict. The following behaviors are referred to as calming signals because they are used to help dogs calm themselves and others in tense situations. Observing these signals will help you to recognize when your dog is stressed.

Mouth In general, a softly closed or slightly opened mouth indicates the dog is relaxed, and a tightly closed mouth indicates tension. Lips that are pulled back to expose teeth can be a snarl, a warning gesture to encourage social distance. In this instance, the lip will be lifted baring the teeth slightly or fully. Many dogs also bare their teeth in an appeasement gesture, often called a submissive grin. Rather than signaling a threat, this expression is meant to deflect hostility. Superficially, it may seem like a snarl, but in this case, the mouth is open and lips are pulled back, almost like a human smile. The dog's entire demeanor will signal friendliness and submission, in contrast with the body language accompanying a defensive snarl.

19

Yawning Dogs yawn when they are tired. But, excessive or repetitive yawning may also be a way to relieve stress.

Lip Licking Dogs normally lick their lips to activate scent receptors, or when eating. But, quick flicks of the tongue over the lips may convey the message that the dog is experiencing tension or stress.

Panting Dogs regulate body temperature primarily by panting (to release body heat). But, panting can also indicate anxiety or stress.

Sniffing Dogs normally sniff the ground to obtain information, but they also resort to this behavior to defuse tension. For example, a dog may

do this when confronted by another dog, or when called by a frustrated owner who is yelling at him.

Ears For some dogs, ear carriage is a good indicator of intention and mood. Ears perked up and forward indicate interest and concentration. Ears held lower than normal may indicate concern or lack of confidence. However, this is dependent on the shape and size of the dog's ears. Long, heavy ears are less mobile. Heavily coated ears cannot be seen as easily.

Eyes Direct, prolonged eye contact is generally avoided in the canine community because it is considered a threatening signal. Dogs usually avert their gaze and blink to signal a non-threatening intent. Avoiding direct eye contact with a stressed or fearful dog is imperative for them to feel less threatened. A dog that is extremely stressed or anxious may also exhibit what is known as "whale eye." The head is still, but the eyes move, showing whites around the edges.

Head A head held high indicates confidence and in some cases the intent to be confrontational. A lowered head may indicate lack of confidence, or the desire to avoid confrontation. For dogs, a head-on approach can be interpreted as a challenge, especially when paired with direct eye contact. Young children often run up to dogs in this manner. Although it is an impulsive, friendly gesture, many dogs instinctively react with fear. Well-socialized adult dogs rarely approach each other this way. Instead, they approach in an arc, stand side to side, and sniff each other rear to head.

Paws Puppies paw their dams to solicit food and paw their littermates to solicit play. As a pup matures, pawing is used to solicit play and attention. It is also a gesture of deference, appeasement, or sexual signaling. In

general, any bending of the elbow and lifting of paws is a friendly or solicitous gesture.

Play Bow One of the most easily identifiable canine gestures is the play bow. A rear in the air and elbows toward the ground signal an invitation to play.

Tails This aspect of canine body language is most commonly misunderstood. It cannot be accurately used to read a dog's emotional state without evaluating the whole picture. Some tail types do not readily communicate canine intentions, such as very short or tightly curled tails.

When the tail is held in its natural position and wags softly, it generally signals that all is well. A tail carried high and wagging quickly indicates tension and excitement. If it happens to be paired with a stiff, forward-tilting body and tensely closed mouth, this is not a dog you want to approach.

Scratching, Stretching, and Shaking Dogs normally scratch to relieve an itch, stretch to warm up muscles, and shake to remove water from their coats. But, all three of these gestures are also used to relieve stress.

Barking, Whining, and Growling All dogs use their voice to communicate. Barking and whining are often interpreted as threats, which is sometimes true. However, there are many other motivations for barking, whining, and growling. Barking, whining, or growling are used:

- to warn of changes in the environment;
- to express excitement or fear;
- as an outlet for boredom;
- as an invitation to play;
- as an attempt to find pack members;
- to indicate conflict (especially when paired with a retreat and advance body movement when the dog is unsure of the situation but wants to investigate further).

In general, the higher the pitch and the lower the intensity of vocalization the less threatening the intent; vocalizations of high pitch and intensity, on the other hand, are associated with alarm. However, your dog may be expressing multiple intentions, and the best way to determine what these are is to be aware of their overall body language and the context of the situation.

Most growling is meant as a warning. The dog is trying to maintain or increase social distance. The meaning is obvious when a dog growls to prevent someone from taking his bone. But, some soft growls and grunts are intended to be playful. Other cues must be observed in order to differentiate between a playful and threatening growl and bark. For example, if the dog is also play bowing or pawing, the growl is meant to be playful. If his body is stiff, the intent is probably threatening.

In either case, growling should not be punished. This may stop the growling, but it also removes an important early warning signal from your dog's repertoire. Instead, a warning growl should tell you that you need to work on making your dog more comfortable in particular situations.

Stages of Development

For better or worse, dogs change as they mature in response to new experiences and potential challenges. Behavioral changes are usually most dramatic during transitions from puppyhood to adolescence, and then to adulthood. It can be challenging for owners to cope with these developmental stages. Just when you begin to make progress and feel your dog understands what is expected, he reaches the next stage of his life, and his behavior and response to the world changes. For example, an otherwise mild-mannered and sociable puppy may begin growling at people or other animals when he is six to nine months old.

Recognizing and accepting the fact that your dog will need your continuing guidance and support throughout his life will help prevent frustration and stress for both dog and family. If you have built a good foundation for a trusting and cooperative relationship with your dog, these emerging potential behavior issues should be less challenging.

Understanding the dog's general developmental stages will prepare you for what to expect and give you the knowledge to properly manage and teach your dog during each phase of his life.

Puppyhood

Puppies, like other young creatures, are naturally playful, inquisitive, and eager to bond and learn. During this period they have the greatest potential for rapid learning, especially when guided by someone they trust. Every pup's temperament is influenced by genetics, but he is essentially a clean slate; he has few preconceived notions of the world and little experience that could be used to form bad habits. From this perspective, training is simple and straightforward. It can be focused on teaching new, reliable behaviors rather than resolving behavior problems.

Raising a puppy can be a truly wonderful experience, but it also has challenges, including moments of serious frustration (and lack of sleep). Successfully raising a puppy requires a commitment to provide essential training and socialization during his critical learning stage, the first four months of life.

Puppyhood is the time to focus on socialization and instilling the foundation for basic manners. Subsequent training can focus on honing a dog's skills and applying them to real-life situations.

Watch for certain predispositions in a young puppy's character. A puppy's personality forms slowly, but these clues will tell you if he has outstanding temperament traits, such as natural confidence or shyness.

- When encouraged to *come*, does the pup approach quickly, slowly, or move away?
- When you walk away, does the pup tend to follow you?
- Does the pup tend to relax, get excited, or freeze stiffly when he is picked up?
- When the pup enters an unfamiliar environment does he investigate, pause, cautiously approach, or attempt to hide?
- How does he react when exposed to loud noises?

At this age, extreme personality traits can be most easily modified through proper training and socialization.

Adolescence

The onset of adolescence varies, but as a general rule, smaller dogs reach mental and physical maturity earlier. Therefore, an adolescent Chihuahua is likely to be more mature than an Irish Setter or Great Dane of the same age.

PAWS TO CONSIDER

Dog's can think logically, reason, learn from experience, and modify their behavior to influence others. For instance, your dog may present you with a toy to elicit a game of fetch. Although dogs are very smart, they are definitely not capable of complicated planning required for spite and revenge. Dogs live in the moment. It is one of their best qualities. They forgive and forget, rather than bear a grudge or scheme to revenge a past wrong.

Much like a teenager, dogs between the ages of approximately four and nine months may seem more challenging. They are larger and stronger, which makes them more difficult to manage. They are also more energetic, confident, and agile. And, like teenagers, their behavior is influenced by hormonal surges (all the more reason to spay and neuter early).

This can be a frustrating time, and it will require much patience, nurturing, and guidance on your part. Good management and a structured routine will help your dog navigate this transition by making his world more predictable. A "Learn to Earn" program is especially helpful during this period of development.

It will gain your dog's cooperation by leveraging his desire to have access to valued resources.

Adulthood

Adult dogs tend to fall into two categories; those that have benefited from early and ongoing guidance to learn how to behave, and those that have not.

Unfortunately, adult dogs who indulge in what most consider to be inappropriate behaviors, such as eliminating in the home, barking excessively, chewing inappropriate items, digging holes in the yard, raiding the garbage can, and counter surfing are often denied social interactions and freedoms. As a result, they have very few opportunities to learn better habits, and their behavior tends to further deteriorate. Many are ultimately surrendered to shelters, and their chances of finding new homes are small once they are unfairly labeled as problem dogs.

Breed Considerations

We can make fairly accurate predictions about a purebred dog's appearance and behavioral tendencies. But, like a weather report, these predictions are sometimes accurate and other times not so much.

Individual temperament is the product of complex genetic traits and environmental influences. As a result, it can vary tremendously within a breed and even a litter. However, it is still advisable to research a breed's history and typical behavioral tendencies when choosing a dog.

It is even more important to evaluate a particular dog's suitability for your particular family and lifestyle. Each dog is a unique creature with a particular genetic makeup, behavioral tendencies, preferences, and experiences that play a part in their behavior and responsiveness to learning. Likewise, each family has a unique structure and dynamic.

Little Dogs, Big Concerns

Contrary to popular belief, small dogs are not invariably difficult to house-train, nor are they prone to bark excessively or behave aggressively toward people. The typical underlying cause of these behaviors has nothing to do with the dog's size. The culprit is the family's behavior in relation to the dog's size.

Alternately known as the "Napoleon Complex" or "Small Dog Syndrome," this refers to all sorts of ill-mannered and unsafe behaviors that owners of diminutive dogs tolerate and/or encourage. They are the result of inadequate management and training that would be less tolerated from a larger dog.

Owners of puppies sometimes indulge in this permissiveness, allowing behaviors such as nipping and jumping because they consider it cute and harmless. Unfortunately, when the dog is an adult, he is reprimanded for the same unruly behavior that has been rewarded for many months. The dog not only becomes very confused, but the habit is now ingrained and difficult to revise.

This permissive approach is often more extreme in the case of small-breed puppies. They are coddled and pampered with little regard for their ultimate behavior as adults. Aggression is often allowed to get completely out of hand simply because of their small size. However, small dogs can inflict serious bites. Without proper training and socialization they are also more likely to become fearful and defensive because of their size disadvantage. Regardless of a dog's size, compliant and mannerly behavior should always be encouraged.

27

Positive Training

Over the past 25 years, advances in the understanding of how dogs learn has resulted in countless trainers and pet parents embracing positive techniques to help them shape healthy and well-behaved dogs.

At a time when our dogs have become family members, positive training is particularly appropriate, as the goal is to create a dog that is mannerly as well as friendly, social, and happy. People of all ages and temperaments can easily master this approach, and there is no requirement for strength or courage in the face of retaliatory aggression that more physical, punishment-based techniques require.

While we will go deeply into the specific mechanics of teaching in other chapters, it is helpful to understand the underlying tenets of positive training. What do we mean by positive? Why is this approach so successful? And why employ it to the exception of all others?

What does it mean to take a positive approach? To answer that, first we have to define the word "positive."

In the broadest sense of the word, "positive" means never losing sight of the simple fact that our dogs deserve to be treated with kindness and consideration for their way of seeing the world, their needs, and the manner in which they are most easily able to learn to adapt and thrive. The main tenet of a positive approach is striving to do no harm and avoiding coercion or fear. Aside from being unkind, creating a fearful state of mind means the dog is far less receptive to learning.

"Positive" is also applied in reference to both reinforcements and punishments, which can make things a bit confusing. In this context, "positive" refers to *applying* or *giving* something to the animal in an effort to enable learning. An example of positive reinforcement is giving a food treat after a behavior occurs to make it more likely to happen again. An example of positive punishment is giving an electric shock after a behavior occurs to make it less likely to happen again. The latter and anything of that ilk is strongly discouraged.

In the context of training, "positive" refers to a training protocol that relies on utilizing positive reinforcement designed to encourage learning

TRAINER'S TIP

Positive training minimizes inappropriate behavior in several ways:

Managing your dog's time using tools and techniques designed to foster success and prevent unwanted behaviors.

Motivating your dog's desire to be guided by you and to play the training game.

Teaching your dog in a way that is easy, effective, and efficient in order to instill appropriate behaviors that can be utilized in the dog's daily life.

Creating Consequences for inappropriate behaviors that help to curb them in the future without side effects.

in a safe, stress-free manner, and shunning positive punishment. However, positive training encompasses more than just teaching dogs through positive reinforcement. It involves gentle management tools and techniques to prevent dogs from engaging in unwanted behaviors. It also emphasizes the importance of mental and physical exercise for a dog's well-being.

Positive training also includes consequences for inappropriate behavior, but these are carefully considered to further the goal of teaching the dog to forgo inappropriate behavior, and to minimize the potential for negative side effects.

Management Magic

One of the simplest tools to prevent or resolve behavior issues is to manage your dog's time in order to prevent unwanted behaviors. Minimizing your dog's opportunities to engage in unwanted behavior has three benefits. First, it decreases his opportunities to practice this activity such that it becomes a fine-tuned habit. Second, by preventing the rewards he expected from this behavior (even if you allowed him access to them unintentionally, such as people talking to him when he jumps), his incentive to continue the habit is also curtailed. Third, it eliminates the potential use of punishments that may have negative side effects.

Management also allows you to focus your energy on teaching appropriate behaviors and rewarding your dog for a job well done. For example, if your dog is jumping on someone, rather than using a more traditional approach like yelling at or otherwise punishing your dog, you can manage the situation by keeping your dog on his leash and holding it or stepping on it to prevent the jumping. Then you can reward polite behavior such as sitting.

Management can be interpreted in many ways. In some cases, it requires no more than providing your dog with a chew toy to keep him occupied and prevent inappropriate chewing. Management might also include the following:

- Keep your dog on a leash for additional control and supervision while he plays. The leash can also be held or tethered to a stable object while your dog plays with a toy.
- Step on your dog's leash to stop him from jumping when he greets people (until he has learned to sit politely for a greeting).
- Confine your dog to a crate for short periods of time to prevent elimination in the home (until he is reliably housetrained).
- Use a head halter or front-clip harness to prevent pulling and lunging on the leash (until he has learned to walk nicely by your side).

PAWS TO CONSIDER

Encouraging Appropriate Behavior Choices

A puppy or untrained adult dog entering your home is not likely to engage in many behaviors that would meet with your approval. Eliminating whenever and wherever they choose, chewing anything that catches their interest, barking and whining, taking food from counters, jumping on people, and play biting aren't high on anyone's list of desirable behaviors. However, from a dog's perspective, they are all perfectly normal behaviors. Your goal is to manage your dog and funnel his energy toward acceptable behaviors. After a while, these will become a habit for your dog, and he will consistently make these choices.

Many pet parents fail to use appropriate management for their dogs due to a misguided guilt about hindering their dog's quality of life. For example, a crate is a fantastic management tool, but many people feel guilty about leaving their dog in a crate, especially when they are home. When used appropriately

and thoughtfully, management tools actually enhance your dog's life. They encourage the dog to make better behavior choices. Eventually, this means that he will be able to enjoy far more freedom and as many privileges as possible. On the other hand, inadequate management allows the dog to engage far more in unsafe, inappropriate behavior. This not only leads to bad habits—it can also place your dog in many dangerous situations. It can aptly be described as "killing with kindness."

Management Tools

Leashes A leash is one of the most obvious canine management tools, yet many pet parents don't make full use of it. In addition to using it to encourage mannerly behavior and keep your dog under control during walks, it's also an effective management tool indoors. Keeping your dog on a leash in the house makes it much easier to supervise his activities and interrupt unwanted behavior. Use this method until you feel confident that he can enjoy freedom in the home without being destructive or getting hurt.

You should have two leashes at your disposal, one for walks and one for indoor management (see information on tethering below). A third, lightweight canvas long line of 15 to 30 feet (4.5 to 9 meters) for future outdoor distance work is also recommended.

Leashes as Tethers A tether is a short leash (4 to 6 feet, or 1.2 to 1.8 meters) attached to a stable object (i.e., an eye-hook in the wall, or a sturdy piece of furniture). Use it to temporarily restrain your dog while he is under supervision. It will:

- help him learn to settle down in the home;
- encourage him to focus on appropriate chew toys;
- prevent inappropriate behaviors (such as jumping on guests);
- act as a useful time-out for inappropriate and/or unruly behavior; and
- keep him out of harm's way until he learns the house rules.

Tethering is especially important for puppies. Allowing a young dog to wander freely around your home will guarantee that you will spend plenty of time cleaning up after him. It also gives him plenty of opportunities to practice inappropriate behaviors and get into potentially harmful situations.

Follow these steps when teaching your dog to tolerate tethering:

1. Attach the tether to your dog and offer him a food-stuffed toy or a treat while standing or sitting next to him.
2. Take a step or two away and then return.
3. Gradually increase the distance you step away. If your dog seems concerned and is not focusing on the toy or treat, remain nearby until he is calm enough to enjoy his toy.
4. Practice tethering your dog in different locations around your home and gradually introduce distractions (eating food, opening doors, holding other toys). This will help him learn to tolerate tethering in the presence of family and visitors who may do all of these things.

Chew Toys Providing your dog with interesting chew toys will prevent countless behavior problems. Whenever you expect your dog to keep himself entertained, provide at least two toys (see more details on choosing appropriate chew toys in Chapter Four on page 62). Every dog loves to chew, and

he will happily focus his energy on this activity without any need for company if you choose toys your dog most prefers. Without the distraction of chew toys he will probably entertain himself by barking excessively, chewing your valuable possessions, or devoting himself to another equally destructive pastime.

Gates and Exercise Pens Gates and exercise pens can be used in a kitchen, bathroom, or mudroom to create a temporary enclosure. This limits your dog's access to parts of your home that pose a risk to him—or your possessions. Choose an area where he cannot inflict chewing damage to furniture, cabinets, or molded baseboards.

Pet-proof the area by removing potential hazards. When your dog is confined in this manner, he should have some safe chew toys to keep him occupied. In some cases (i.e., for puppies) you should also cover the floor with absorbent housetraining pads (see Chapter Five, page 94, for more details).

Crates A properly sized crate is an invaluable management tool for housetraining; it helps to prevent inap-

propriate chewing and teaches your dog to spend some quiet time alone. It is also useful as an aid to keep your dog safe while traveling in the car or when your dog needs to be safely confined (such as when you have a repair person in your home). Introduce him to the crate gradually and use it exclusively for short-term confinement (see Chapter Five on page 87 for more details).

PAWS TO CONSIDER

Dog Proofing

You must be thorough when pet-proofing your home for your dog's safety. If there is a way for him to do something inappropriate in his enclosed area, he will find it. Carefully check the entire space, looking for possible ways that he can get hurt or engage in undesirable behaviors, such as chewing inappropriate items. Make sure to correct *all* the potential problems—not *most* of them.

Motivating Your Dog to Play the Training Game: "Learn to Earn"

Most people give their dog a scratch behind the ear, a kind word, or a treat to reward a job well done. Both humans and animals quickly learn to repeat behaviors that result in something they consider rewarding. Those behaviors are more likely to be repeated in order to increase the likelihood of a reward. This is what positive reinforcement is all about. For instance, employers provide paychecks for the work we do, and sometimes offer bonuses for exceptionally good work. Coaches and teachers motivate with praise, good grades, and awards.

How do we apply these principles to teach our dog that being respectful and mannerly is the fastest route to what they want (i.e., food, toys, attention, access to fun environments)? It's as easy as "Learn to Earn."

Considering the enormity of the task that we ask our dogs to accomplish (abiding by our rules to keep them safe, healthy, and happy) it makes sense to use *all* of the things your dog values when motivating him to play the training game. Rewards strengthen the behaviors you want from your dog. But, both rewards and reward removal can work as powerful motivators in this game.

So, put on your coaching cap and step into the role of your dog's leader in the "Learn to Earn" program. Basically, this consists of teaching your dog to respond to a simple request such as "*Sit*," praising his cooperation, and following this up with something else he wants. This can include an almost endless list of potential rewards: food, a bowl of water, opening the front door to head out for a walk, inviting him on the couch, giving him a belly rub, or allowing him to play with another dog. You're going to offer your dog all of these things anyway, so why not do so in a way that contributes to his education as a compliant, mannerly dog? Ask your dog to exert a bit of effort and respond to your requests in order to earn his rewards. He will quickly figure out that you are the source of all the good things he wants in life, and he will acknowledge you as his kind, compassionate coach. From there, you can continue to guide him toward success using motivation and love.

TRAINER'S TIP

Earning a Paycheck

Get into the habit of asking your dog to do a little something in exchange for the things he wants. This can become part of your daily routine as you feed him, walk him, or offer him a new toy. He will perceive you as his leader in the best sense of the word, and he will become a mannerly canine companion who respects his relationship with people.

Growling when a toy is about to be taken away, barking incessantly, jumping on people, and ignoring house rules characterize dogs that haven't received guidance regarding appropriate behavior. They also clearly make no connection between the source of their well-being and the people they currently growl at and ignore. These dogs have insufficient understanding of earning what they want from their people.

Techniques for Teaching Behaviors

There is a saying that "everything you train your dog to do, he already knows perfectly." For instance, your dog certainly knows how to *sit, lie down, stand*, retrieve objects, etc. One of the major goals of training is to help your dog to learn to make a connection between words and behaviors such that he responds reliably when you ask him to do things.

There are many advantages to teaching your dog to perform behaviors on cue or request.

- Teaching him to *sit* on cue means you can ask him to greet people politely (a wonderful alternative to jumping).
- Teaching your dog to *lie down* on cue means you can ask him to remain on his bed when you are eating (a wonderful alternative to begging at the table).

PAWS TO CONSIDER

Rewards as Magnificent Motivators

Great trainers are wonderful pet detectives. They make a point of discovering everything that motivates their dogs. Every dog has slightly different preferences. Your dog may be especially motivated by a special treat, a walk, or a favorite toy. These become his high-priority rewards. Always be sure he does something to earn a high-priority reward. This will teach him impulse control and good manners, and will help to deter inappropriate behaviors.

- Teaching your dog to *come when called* means you can ask him to return to you (a wonderful alternative to running off and possibly getting lost or hurt).
- Teaching your dog to *drop* something on cue means you can safely take items away from him (a wonderful alternative to struggling with a growling dog to stop him from ingesting something potentially harmful).

There are five approaches to eliciting behaviors so they can be put on cue. Every method has pros and cons, and some have more of one than the other. It is generally preferable to use capturing, luring, shaping, or targeting rather than physical molding.

Regardless of the method of choice, each requires the use of a "marker" (a sound like the word "*Yes!*" or the click of a clicker) that becomes associated with a reward. Following the marker sound with a reward helps your dog form a link between that behavior and the possibility of a reward. This process can be compared to a detailed, highly focused snapshot of the behavior that helps your dog easily understand exactly why he is being rewarded.

Targeting, luring, and molding are techniques used to prompt or guide the dog into a desired position. Capturing and shaping rely on the dog offering behaviors with little prompting from the trainer (other than marking and rewarding for what they want).

Rewarding for the complete desired behavior is known as capturing. For example, when working on *sit*, you would wait for your dog to do so, and then mark and reward. In this case, you have effectively captured the behavior and made it more likely that your dog will offer it again.

Shaping rewards incremental steps toward the desired behavior. For example, when working on a behavior such as teaching your dog to circle, you would mark and reward for gradually increasing turns in one direction until the dog understands that a full circle is what is expected.

Quest for Quiet: Adding Verbal Cues to Training

Language is our primary means of communication, and since we have such high expectations of our dogs' ability to understand what we are saying, it's easy to assume they do. They are very good at interpreting our intentions, but this isn't quite the same as understanding human language. Dogs certainly

How to Add a Verbal Cue to a Learned Behavior

Much of training involves teaching your dog to make connections between cues, requests, or commands and specific behaviors, and to respond reliably to them in a variety of situations. This is referred to as putting a behavior under stimulus (or cue) control.

It's best to begin to add a verbal cue in a controlled environment with few distractions when your dog is reliably offering the desired behavior, or when he is responding to a lure or target. This ensures that he will make a clear connection between the word and the behavior.

When you begin this process, your dog is likely to offer a newly reinforced behavior many times in an effort to get as many rewards as possible. That is very encouraging, but eventually, he must learn that certain behaviors will earn rewards when they are performed on request.

Say the cue word just before the behavior is about to happen. Needless to say, this requires observation skills and timing. If you are capturing or shaping a behavior, observe your dog's body language for signs that he is about to offer the behavior or something close to it. If you are luring or targeting, say the word just prior to moving your hand to lure or target your dog into position. Mark and reward for the behavior.

During this phase of training, you must also ignore your dog when he offers the behavior without the cue. This is an important part of your dog learning that the behavior is rewarded when requested.

It will require many repetitions in brief three- to five-minutes sessions before your dog makes a connection. When you are confident that your dog has made the connection, say the cue word before he shows the first indication of offering the behavior. Once he has mastered that big step you can begin practicing this sequence in other areas of your home and eventually try it outdoors to develop reliability in various environments.

vocalize to communicate (e.g., yelping, growling, barking, and howling), but body language is much more important to their complex communication system.

Because of this major discrepancy in our communication systems, we must restrict our verbalizing, especially during the initial stages of training. Otherwise, your dog is likely to suffer from information overload as he tries to understand your every word and gesture. Too much talking is likely to confuse him, and as a result, he may give up and tune you out.

Basically, there is no point in adding words to a behavior until your dog understands a new training concept (i.e., what behavior you want). When you are confident that he understands what is expected, you can add a verbal cue, request, or command to the behavior. This way he gradually learns to link the word with the particular behavior.

Capturing

Capturing takes advantage of opportunities when your dog performs desirable behaviors on his own by pinpointing them with a marker. For instance, if your dog happens to lie down in front of you, immediately let him know that this earns a reward by marking and rewarding that behavior. The dog is likely to repeat the same behavior in hopes of earning another reward. When the dog begins to offer the behavior reliably, you can say a verbal cue just before he does it. Repeating this sequence helps your dog make an association between the word and the behavior.

In trainer's terms these are the ABC's of learning:

- Antecedent: The cue or command.
- Behavior: What the dog does.
- Consequence: The reward.

Capturing a Behavior and Putting it on Cue

Teaching the *Sit* Command

1. Hold a handful of tiny treats and stand silently near your dog. Ignore any behaviors other than sitting.
2. When he *sits*, mark the behavior and offer him a treat from your hand or toss it on the ground.
3. Take a step away and wait for your dog to *sit* again. When he does, repeat the sequence of marking and rewarding the behavior.
4. After five to ten repetitions, your dog is likely to have a light-bulb moment and realize that you want him to *sit*. At this point he will do so more promptly.
5. When you are confident that your dog will *sit* when you take a step away and stop, say "*Sit*" immediately when you stop.

6. When he *sits*, mark the behavior and give him an extra treat to end the session on a high note.

Capturing Pros:

- Capturing is one of the easiest methods you can use to teach simple behaviors that your dog is likely to offer on his own: making eye contact, sitting, lying down, standing, or heading in your direction (*come when called*).
- When a trainer develops good timing and observation skills, other behaviors become easier to capture as well, such as taking a bow, sneezing, and circling.
- Capturing is also a great way for your dog to become an extremely thoughtful participant in the training game.

Capturing Cons:

- Capturing requires good timing and observation skills, which may take some practice to develop.
- If you or your dog is new to capturing, the initial sessions may be somewhat discouraging.
- For beginners, sessions should be frequent but brief. This way, you and your dog are more likely to have fun learning this new way to communicate.

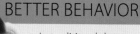

BETTER BEHAVIOR

In traditional dog training, correction was a polite term for punishment. Positive training methods help your dog choose better behavior options. If your dog does something you don't like, calmly interrupt him and help him refocus on an alternate activity. For example, if your dog is chewing on your shoe, calmly pick up his leash (which should be attached to him since he is in the training process), lead him away from it, hold the leash away from you, and ignore him for a minute (for a time-out). Then offer him an appropriate chew toy. This way he learns that chewing shoes results in a time-out and practices the better behavior of chewing a toy. This assumes that the alternative behavior is at least as rewarding as the inappropriate one.

Shaping

Shaping can be compared to the "hot and cold" game. One person chooses a behavior or a location, and the other player tries to guess what this is. "Hot" lets them know they are getting closer to the goal and "cold" tells them they are getting further away from it.

When shaping behavior, you use a marker (either a clicker or a word) to let him know when his choices are getting closer (or "hot") to the response that you want. This method reinforces tiny approximations or steps toward the desired goal behavior. Both the marker sound and the absence of it give your dog information. The sound of the marker tells your dog, *"Yes, you did something right"* ("hot") and the absence of a marker sound indicates, *"that wasn't the right choice, try something else"* ("cold").

When using this technique, every mark or click must be followed by a treat. Dogs need a lot of information or feedback when we are shaping a behavior. Think of it as a game played in baby steps. If you wait too long between clicks (or verbal marks) your dog may find the game too difficult and give up. Shaping is especially useful for teaching complex behavior sequences, such as opening a box and putting a toy inside of it, or going to a particular spot and lying down. The amount of time needed to teach a new behavior through shaping can vary. This depends on the trainer's timing and overall skills, the dog's temperament, and past experiences of being reinforced for problem solving during training. Dogs and trainers that are savvy about shaping can learn new behaviors with amazing speed.

Shaping a Behavior

Learning to Put Both Paws Up on a Low Stool

1. When the dog looks at the stool, click and reward him.
2. Click and reward him when he moves a paw toward the stool.
3. If his paw makes contact with the stool, click and reward. (Each time you reward him toss the treat several inches away so he will have the opportunity to reapproach the stool).
4. Click and reward him when he places a paw on the stool.
5. Click and reward him when he places both paws on the stool.
6. When you are confident that your dog understands that you want him to put both paws on the stool, begin adding a verbal cue such as *"Step up"* immediately before he does it.
7. At this point, begin ignoring the dog when he steps up onto the stool unless you have asked him to do it. This way he will learn that the rewards are earned by performing this behavior when requested.

CHECKLIST

Qualities of a Great Dog Trainer

How you choose to teach your dog affects the ease, efficiency, and reliability of attaining your training goals. In addition to using a gentle and compassionate approach, setting realistic expectations, and adhering to a "Learn to Earn" program, these tips will help you become a great trainer.

Great trainers...

✓ engage in a relationship that encourages the dog to trust them and look to them for guidance.

✓ manage their dog so that the easiest behavior choice to make is the right one.

✓ have a strong understanding of the underlying principles of canine learning.

✓ identify the things their dog finds rewarding and use these as a leverage to reinforce desired behaviors.

✓ focus on rewarding behaviors they like rather than punishing the dog for misbehaving.

✓ provide information and motivation by telling the dog what to do and by giving him a reason to do it.

✓ acknowledge that many factors in a dog's life impact each behavior.

✓ master their emotions and remain calm when faced with potential training frustrations.

✓ refrain from verbal requests until the dog develops a physical understanding of the task and reliably demonstrates the correct performance response.

8. You can also practice this sequence from different positions in relation to your dog and the stool so he will learn to respond regardless of positioning.

Shaping Pros:
- This is a superb technique for teaching complex behaviors.
- It helps trainers sharpen their timing and observation skills.
- Shaping opens the door to a range of fun, creative training goals.

Shaping Cons:
- Shaping requires good observational and mechanical skills, which come with practice.
- Dogs that have been subjected to punishment-based techniques may be reluctant to offer new behaviors (as they may suffer from a sort of overall suppression of activity).

Luring

Luring consists of calling the dog's attention to something in your hand, such as a tiny food treat or a toy that can be tossed as a reward. While holding this item, move your hand to guide the dog into desired positions. Within ten to twenty repetitions in a session your dog will start to move more smoothly and promptly into the position you are working on as he begins to associate the hand movement with the desired position and the resulting reward.

Luring a Dog to Sit

1. Show the dog that you have a treat in your hand and hold it at the level of his nose.
2. Slowly move your hand slightly up and back over your dog's head.
3. As his head moves up, his rear moves toward the floor (sort of like a see-saw), and he will sit.
4. Mark the moment his rear hits the floor and follow it up with a reward.
5. When you are confident your hand movement will cause the behavior to happen, you can add the cue word (in this case, "*Sit*") just prior to moving your hand.
6. With repetition, your dog will learn to respond to the cue word as he did with the hand movement/lure.

Phasing Out Lures

Lures can be a valuable part of training because they provide an extremely efficient and effective way to elicit behaviors and teach the dog the relevance of responding to us (i.e., the lure becomes a reward). However, since you don't want to have to rely on a food or toy lure to get your pup to respond, you must be sure to phase out the use of the lure so your dog's behavior is not contingent upon them in the long term. Phasing out the use of a lure means your dog will eventually respond reliably to hand and verbal cues without your holding a treat or toy.

1. Hold a lure in your hand to elicit the behavior, but reward him for following the lure with a treat from the other hand. Repeat this ten to twenty times.
2. After a few sessions like this, make the same lure movement without a treat in that hand; instead, hold and offer the treat as a reward from the other. In this way your dog is responding to the empty-handed signal as opposed to the food or toy lure (which has now become solely a reward).

3. Practice the empty-handed signal and reward with a treat from your pocket or a nearby countertop.
4. Practice the empty-handed signal and substitute the food reward with a variety of alternatives, such as tossing a toy or opening the front door for a walk.

Luring Pros:
- Luring is a fast way to elicit certain behaviors, specifically body positions such as *sit, down,* and *stand.*
- As a result, both dog and trainer are reinforced with success from the start.
- It is relatively easy to learn the mechanics of luring. Even young children can play this game with a dog (with adult supervision).
- It instills in your dog the concept of responding to hand signals, which is an essential tool for controlling your dog from a distance.
- Luring teaches dogs to enjoy hands moving around them (this is especially useful for timid dogs).

Luring Cons:
- Luring should be used to elicit a specific behavior or body position and should be phased out quickly to prevent the dog from responding reliably only when he sees a treat.
- Some people have difficulty mastering the mechanics of phasing out lures, and understanding how to do this is crucial to the process.

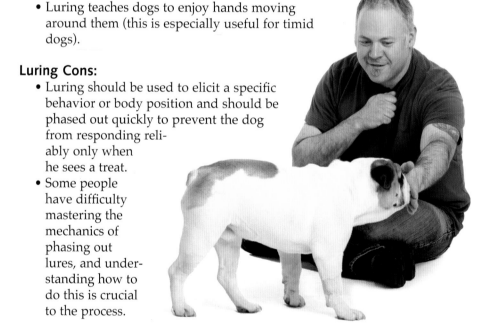

Targeting
Targeting teaches your dog to touch a chosen object with a designated body part (such as your hand) or object (such as a target stick) on cue. This comes in handy in many situations, such as teaching your dog to touch people's hands to say hello. In more advanced training, targeting is often used to train service dogs to turn light switches on or off or to manipulate door handles.

For the average dog owner, targeting has many practical uses. It is an easy way to move your dog from one spot to another because he will follow your hand. It's also a good foundation for teaching a dog to *come when called* because you can train him to target to your hand from a greater distance. Targeting is also a helpful technique to prevent or resolve hand shyness because it teaches the dog that touching a hand with his nose can be highly rewarding. It's also a good way to redirect and refocus a dog's attention. Teaching your dog to touch the end of a stick or dowel is useful when teaching him to walk nicely on leash. (See page 133 for more information on targeting.)

Targeting Pros:
- Targeting is an easy way to direct your dog (for example, off the furniture or onto a table at the veterinarian or groomer). This is especially handy for owners of large dogs.
- Dogs respond more easily to visual rather than verbal cues.
- Targeting can be used as a basis to teach countless complex behaviors.
- It is a very easy skill to master and therefore a great confidence booster for you and your dog.

Targeting Cons:
None, other than the fact that once you start, you may become addicted to this fun and useful training method!

Molding

Molding uses physical manipulation to elicit behaviors or body positions. Examples of this technique include applying pressure to the dog's rear to make him sit, or pushing on his shoulders to make him lie down.

Molding Pros:
- It is easy for people to understand the concept since the mechanics of it are obvious.

Molding Cons:
- Many dogs resist being physically manipulated, and this can make them dislike the training experience.
- Physically pushing and pulling a fearful or timid dog can cause him to become defensive and growl, snap, or even bite.
- Molding requires a degree of physical strength, which can be problematic for some trainers, especially children or the elderly.
- Pushing a dog into a position may elicit the opposition reflex, causing him to instinctively resist the pressure and try to maintain his balance.
- Molding doesn't encourage your dog to learn verbal cues because he will focus on the potentially unpleasant physical contact.
- This method doesn't provide any ability to control the dog when he is outside your physical reach.

Curbing Unwanted Behaviors

Most people approach training with the main goal of eliminating behaviors they consider inappropriate, rather than teaching their dog to *do* the things they want. Curbing unwanted behaviors involves a combination of managing your dog's time in order to minimize opportunities to practice unwanted behaviors, and teaching him appropriate behaviors to replace unwanted habits. For example, teach your dog to *sit* to say hello instead of wildly jumping on guests to greet them.

There are also ways to let your dog know that certain actions will result in negative consequences. However, these consequences must be carefully considered to avoid potential negative side effects. Yelling, hitting, or otherwise hurting or frightening your dog is obviously not going to enhance his motivation to learn, nor does it bode well for your relationship with your dog.

Reinforcers (anything your dog likes) are used to strengthen behaviors, but they can also be leveraged to decrease unwanted behaviors by removing access to them when an unwanted behavior is occurring. Removing an opportunity for rewards or access to fun activities is known as negative punishment because you are negating or taking away rewards. It lets your dog know that a specific behavior has undesirable consequences—from his

BREAKING THE HABIT

Curbing Play Nipping

Typically, after a few days of low-key adjustment most pups gain confidence, and it is all about full steam ahead puppy enthusiasm, investigation, and play. Much of this includes investigating and playing through the use of their mouths. The result can be arms and hands covered in marks caused by razor-sharp puppy teeth. A common response is to grab the pup's mouth and hold it shut while saying something like "No biting!" This sort of technique is likely to make the situation worse and to cause normal puppy mouthing to turn into growling and aggressive snapping.

The first step is to inhibit the pup's force of mouthing and then frequency (that is, to eliminate mouthing altogether). The reason for this gradual, two-step approach is that in order for a pup to grow into a safe adult dog (a dog that does not inflict injury to people through biting), he needs to nip in order to get feedback about just how delicate human skin is. That way, if he ever were to bite as an adult dog (for example, if someone accidentally stepped on his tail), he would inflict little or no harm.

Observing how a pup spends the first eight weeks of his life, with his mother and littermates, provides insight into the most effective means of teaching bite inhibition. This is when he begins to learn social skills including inhibiting the force of his bite. If he bites too hard the other dogs will yelp and move away, which will temporarily eliminate the pup's access to the mother's milk or to play with littermates. Similarly, keeping your pup on leash during supervised play allows you to hold him gently at arm's length for a time-out from interacting with you or having access to run around and play.

The time-out should last about ten to thirty seconds, at which point you can resume play. Be prepared to give plenty of time-outs, as it will take lots of repetitions for your pup to learn that excessive and rough nipping means he loses playtime with you. Unlike grabbing the dog's muzzle or yelling at him, this method has no undesirable side effects. It simply makes the following point: if you bite me, play is over.

Additionally, be considerate of the fact that a pup needs an outlet for his desire to mouth and chew. Access to safe chew toys is important for the lifelong physical and mental health of your dog. But, it is especially important during puppyhood when your pup's gums are tender due to adult teeth growing in.

It is also wise to give your pup plenty of time to rest throughout the day. While rigorous, prolonged play periods may tire your puppy out, they might also over-stimulate him. An overtired pup tends to have a harder time showing self-control, especially in regard to mouthing. So, be sure your pup has plenty of time to rest in between playtimes.

perspective. This is also sometimes referred to as a time-out.

Negative Punishment

Time-out A time-out is a good example of a negative punishment. This gives your dog an opportunity to learn that the behavior he was engaged in has resulted in his privileges being temporarily revoked. This tool helps to set clear boundaries so your dog can understand what is acceptable and what is not. Think of time-outs in organized sports like hockey.

A few behaviors that respond well to time-outs are attention seeking barking, jumping up, and begging at the table.

TRAINER'S TIP

Effective time-outs should be brief (usually a minute or so) and usually need to be repeated several times for the dog to make a clear connection between the behavior and the consequence. The number of repetitions needed before a dog understands this concept varies. This depends on several factors:

- Behavior patterns: If the dog has been allowed to engage in this behavior for years, he will likely need far more time to adjust to the idea of revising his habits.
- Environment: Competing stimulation in your dog's environment may distract him from the issue at hand.
- Good timing: The time-out must happen as an immediate consequence of the unwanted behavior for the dog to link the events. At the same time, you must maintain a calm, patient approach as you help your dog grasp the idea that he is experiencing a time-out from fun.

The exact nature of a time-out depends on the circumstance. Some time-outs can be at the end of a leash, and others may be where your dog is removed to a location that is sufficiently remote from the area where he's been getting into trouble. This should be a fairly accessible spot so you can administer a time-out quickly and repeatedly if needed. A time-out area 20 yards (18.29 meters) away won't work. You will need at least ten seconds to him get there, and by then, he may not connect his behavior with the consequences. Keeping him on a leash will prevent him from trying the "catch me if you can" game. You can easily call *Time-out* simply by slipping his leash handle on a doorknob or other stable object a few feet away. Holding his leash at arm's length and ignoring him can also be an effective time-out. You can also issue a time-out by calmly walking him to his crate or long-term confinement area, such as an exercise pen.

Positive Punishment

A punishment is something aversive or unpleasant that the dog experiences during or after an event in order to stop a behavior.

Needless to say, few people want a relationship with their dog based on threats and pain. Yet many owners resort to positive punishment out of frustration. More worrisome is the fact that this type of punishment is often reinforcing to the punisher, as it is often an effective means of immediately stopping a dog's unwanted behavior. Instant results are alluring, particularly when you are annoyed or frustrated. Unfortunately, the use of positive punishments has very limited long-term effects and many potential negative side effects.

Punishments like this may temporarily interrupt a behavior, but this deceptively quick fix doesn't teach the dog *what to do* instead and often creates more complicated behavior issues. A dog can be frightened and

TRAINING TRUTH

Your Dog's Guilty Conscience

Many owners believe that their dogs know when they have done something wrong and therefore deserve to be punished. In reality, a dog's guilty look is a response to fear and stress of impending punishment. Perhaps you come home to find the garbage can tipped over once again. Your dog is hiding in the corner with his ears flattened and his tail tucked. He may look like a crook caught red-handed. However, a dog would interpret this body posture as a desire to deflect an impending hostile interaction. Your dog probably knows what's coming because you have done a good job training him to make this connection. You regularly find the trash strewn about the house and react by verbally or physically reprimanding him.

This approach often results in your dog potentially becoming mistrustful, scared, and confused. He may have done this five hours ago and hasn't given it a thought since then. Dogs live in the moment. Unlike us, they do not scrutinize past events or contemplate complicated situations. His five-minute crime spree may have resulted in trash all over the house and your subsequent anger, but this chain of events is too complex for him to understand.

On the other hand, he has probably formed a clear link between your arrival and his punishment. Therefore, your dog will most likely learn to expect punishment when you come home, rather than connecting it to the garbage raid.

There are better ways to confront this problem. Perhaps your dog is bored, stressed, or hungry. Instead of allowing this to happen again, manage the situation. Start by keeping the trash out of his reach, then address the underlying cause of his behavior. If he is bored, provide food-stuffed toys to keep him busy when you are gone. If you forget to take care of these things and your dog once again has a trash party in your absence, hold yourself responsible. You now know how to manage the problem. Train yourself to do a better job next time.

traumatized by forceful training, especially if he is already timid or shy. This can lead to retaliatory or self-defensive aggression or global suppression. The dog will simply shut down and stop responding. At the other end of the spectrum are dogs that become immune to punishment, which encourages even more abusive treatment. Many dogs learn to wait until they are alone and "safe" before indulging in the forbidden behavior.

These scenarios are understandably distasteful to most dog owners. Therefore, the emphasis should be on managing your dog to prevent unwanted behaviors, and rewarding desired behaviors to increase their frequency and strength.

Any potential success that results from a punitive approach isn't justified when humane training is available. An alternative to positive punishment is the *taking away* of something the dog enjoys. This could be access to running around, or simply engaging in the training game, which gives the dog an opportunity to earn what he wants. In this way the dog will learn that a specific behavior results in the loss of what he wants at a given moment.

Principles of Positive Training: Set Your Dog Up to Succeed

In any given situation, your dog has multiple behavior choices. Management allows you to limit his options to choices you consider appropriate. Consistently rewarding him when he makes that choice is also part of the fastest route to success. For example, if your dog is learning to greet people politely (keeping four feet on the floor standing or sitting), keep him on a leash that you can hold or step on to prevent him from jumping. This leaves you free to focus on rewarding him for greeting politely. This technique will strengthen the preferred behavior, and gradually you can phase out the leash greetings as he gets into the habit of reliably sitting or standing still to say hello, which he has learned is the most rewarding option.

Repetition Results in Reliability

In an exercise program, frequent repetitions are needed to build muscle strength, and this also holds true for your dog's behavior or learning muscles. A routine of frequent, brief sessions will improve his ability to make the right choice. Consistently being rewarded for appropriate behavior dramatically increases the odds that he will continue to make the right behavior choices.

Take Tiny Steps Toward Success

In the fast-paced, modern world, we are accustomed to instant results. However, our dogs are not computers, and we must remind ourselves to be patient. Give your dog enough time to process the information you are teaching him. Small steps toward your behavior goals may seem like a snail's pace, but it's the slow and steady trainer and dog teams that are likely to win the race.

Don't Drastically Increase Difficulty

Successful trainers are not in a hurry to increase the difficulty of a training task. Make sure that your dog thoroughly understands what is expected of him before proceeding to the next phase of training. Carefully consider the difficulty of a particular task in terms of duration of the task, the distance you are from your dog, and the degree of distractions in the environment. Asking your dog to accomplish something that is beyond his present level of ability will result in frustration for both of you.

Assumptions Aren't Allowed

Don't assume that your dog knows something even though he has responded in the past. Reliably understanding a behavior is a long-term goal. Reaching that goal requires consistent practice in many contexts. Your dog may sit on command in your living room, but that doesn't guarantee that he will respond the same when you are at the park. Likewise, sitting in your living room becomes an entirely different challenge for your dog if guests are perched on the sofa and a pizza is on the coffee table.

Blame the Trainer, Not the Dog

It's a common misconception to categorize dogs as good or bad. Great trainers take responsibility for their dog's behavior. If your dog isn't doing something you want, consider your approach to teaching this task. Are you overlooking management options that might improve his success? Are you using magnificent motivators and consistently rewarding his progress? Are you introducing new ideas at the right pace as you move forward with his training?

Use It or Lose It

Great trainers give their dogs plenty of opportunities to polish their skills. This keeps the behaviors strong and gives your dog an outlet for his mental and physical energy. Practice sessions also keep your dog happily employed doing things that you want, and leave little time for him to engage in what you consider inappropriate behaviors.

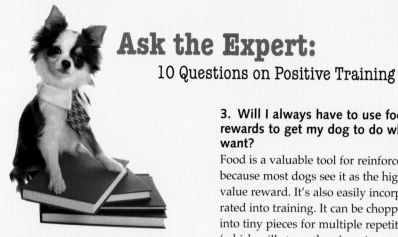

Ask the Expert:
10 Questions on Positive Training

1. Will I ever be able to give my dog freedom, or will he always need a crate, leash, and other management tools?

Once you have built a great relationship with your dog and instilled a strong foundation of good habits, manners, and social skills, you can give your dog access to progressively greater degrees of freedom. But, you should also be prepared to potentially reintroduce these tools if a problem develops.

2. Is it fair to make my dog work for the things he wants? Do I have to make him earn everything?

Putting your dog on a "Learn to Earn" program is the easiest way to use what he wants as leverage to get what you want (i.e., what you consider mannerly behavior). Keep in mind that being on this program isn't so much about limiting the things your dog gets as it is about controlling how and when they are doled out. Plus, your dog doesn't understand that he is on this program. He will simply learn to accept the idea that getting something he wants requires giving you something in exchange. This is a wonderful way to make use of your dog's mental energy and is a fair deal all around that will result in happiness for both you and your dog.

3. Will I always have to use food rewards to get my dog to do what I want?

Food is a valuable tool for reinforcement because most dogs see it as the highest value reward. It's also easily incorporated into training. It can be chopped into tiny pieces for multiple repetitions (which will strengthen learning muscles), and it can be consumed quickly so the next training opportunity can begin as soon as possible. However, food is just one of many things that you can use to reinforce desirable behaviors. Make sure to utilize other things your dog values so he considers *you* important, not just food. For example, you can reward your dog by tossing a toy, allowing him to spend some extra time sniffing on a walk, or inviting him onto the couch.

4. How do I correct my dog when he is doing something wrong so he will understand not to do it again?

In an emergency you may resort to interrupting your dog by using a forceful tone—for example, if your dog has gotten off leash and is in danger. However, that doesn't imply that verbal or physical corrections should be employed as a methodology. There are much safer and more humane options, such as focusing your dog's behavior in the right direction so you don't have to say no. For example, if your dog is jumping on a counter you should consider keeping him on leash when supervised, providing him with chew toys that keep him occupied, and confining him away from the kitchen when you can't supervise him.

5. I keep hearing that I need to be dominant. How do I become my dog's alpha?

Following your guidance and instructions will come naturally if you focus on controlling and leveraging the things your dog values. It is far more effective than confrontational alpha training techniques and does not put your dog at risk of suffering from negative side effects, such as fear, stress, or related aggression.

6. If I don't correct my dog, how will he learn that he has done something wrong?

First of all, "*no*" is not a verb. It doesn't tell your dog what to do, and dogs rely on us to help them understand what we expect of them. Dogs don't perceive things in terms of right or wrong. They do understand the difference between safe and unsafe, and behaviors that are rewarding or non-rewarding. Focus on teaching your dog to seek opportunities to offer rewarding behaviors rather than avoiding those that are unsafe. If he begins perceiving things as unsafe due to punishment, he may become a nervous, jumpy, frightened dog. These aren't qualities anyone wants in a companion dog.

7. When I had a dog as a kid, we used a choke collar and it seemed to work just fine. Why shouldn't I use that now?

Luckily, in the twenty-first century we know much more about how dogs learn. We have better, safer, more humane and effective tools for training. Alternatives to pain-inducing techniques and tools work and have the added benefit of strengthening your bond with your dog. So, the choice is clear. There is no need to choke your dog to teach him when you can simply make use of one or more of the many other options available, such as a front-clip harness, head halter, buckle collar, treats, and other rewards. These will help you gently manage your dog and teach him that walking close by while on leash is rewarding and fun.

8. My dog's breed was developed for protection and I want him to protect our family. Won't all of this treat training make him less of a guard dog?

The foundation of any well-trained protection dog is trust and control. A mannerly and social dog makes a far better protection dog. A dog who reacts constantly to stimuli and is not under your control is a dangerous liability and is potentially unsafe for everyone around him, not just intruders.

9. I just got a new dog, but he is 6 years old. Can this type of training work with an adult rescue dog?

This approach is especially valuable when training an adult rescue dog. He may be experiencing stress adjusting to his new life. Therefore, using a training method that focuses on building trust and cooperation is the best way to motivate his desire to learn, to be guided by you, and to feel secure and confident.

10. I want my kids to be involved in training. Is this sort of training safe for children?

Adults should always supervise interactions between children and dogs. Motivational and reinforcement training is particularly suitable for families with children. It requires no physical coercion or punitive physical corrections. As a training technique, it lowers the risks for potential aggression, because the process of teaching specific behaviors reinforces the dog's association between good things and people.

Training Toolbox

Terms and Tools

The world of canine education has a language of its own, as well as a plethora of potential physical and conceptual tools. Many of them are referenced and recommended throughout this book. Some are commonly mentioned, used, or misused in training classes and on dog training TV shows.

Every method and piece of equipment should be evaluated for safety and effectiveness as you endeavor to guide your dog toward becoming a mannerly and happy companion. Some tools are essential, such as a leash and toys that can be filled with food. Some serve multiple purposes, and many work best when combined with others. For example, a leash prevents your dog from running off and getting hurt. But, it can also be used as a tether to prevent and manage behavior problems such as jumping or begging at the table. It can also be used in combination with a food-stuffed toy to keep your dog happily occupied and out of trouble.

Rewards

Rewards to Reinforce

There is a simple reason why a reward is one of the most effective tools for modifying your dog's behavior. A dog is likely to repeat a behavior that leads to something desirable. Therefore, rewards will strengthen the behavior that precedes it.

Any object or activity that your dog values can be used in this context, as long as the dog receives it immediately after performing the desired action. For example, to strengthen your

BETTER BEHAVIOR

You are not going to be the *only* rewarding thing in your dog's life, but you should be the *most* rewarding. Set the stage for a positive approach to communicating with your dog by leveraging things he wants in exchange for appropriate behavior.

dog's response to sitting on cue, first ask him to perform the behavior. As soon as he complies, use a clicker or say a word such as "yes" to mark the response, immediately followed by a special reward. This could be a special treat or a favorite toy. The expectation of this special reward builds his incentive to sit on cue the next time.

Primary and Secondary Reinforcers

A primary reinforcer, also called an unconditioned reinforcer, is something that your dog will respond to instinctively, like food, water, or reproduction. Dogs are hardwired to respond to primary reinforcers.

Secondary reinforcers, also known as conditioned reinforcers, acquire value when paired with a primary reinforcer, such as food. The clicker

is a good example. The sound it produces will not motivate the dog until he learns to link it with a primary reinforcer. When he makes this connection, he will perceive the click with his expectation of a treat. Verbal praise is another secondary reinforcer. Dogs are not inherently programmed to perceive praise as valuable, but they quickly learn that it is usually combined with high-value rewards.

Identify What Your Dog Finds Rewarding

To be effective, a reward must be sufficiently enticing to motivate a change in your dog's behavior. If your dog truly wants this reward, he will be inspired to work for it. If a particular reward does not intensify your dog's motivation to repeat the behavior, reevaluate. Perhaps he found something more interesting or valuable in the environment, such as a passing dog, an interesting scent, or someone tossing a tennis ball. In this case, you need to reassess the value of the reward you are offering in relation to these distractions, and consider better management to set your dog up to succeed.

Ultimately, your dog will decide what is rewarding to him. Your job is to identify these things and control your dog's access to them. Recognizing what he desires at any time and managing his access to it gives you leverage over his resulting behavior. This concept is at the core of positive training.

Rewards can take many forms. It might be something you offer to your dog, like a treat or the toss of a toy. They can also be things in his environment that you might not recognize as rewarding, such as hunting in a kitty litter box.

Rewards include, but are not limited to:

- Food
- Toys
- Attention
- Access to the environment (This includes everything that is available as a result, such as running about and sniffing, or playing with other dogs.)

The effective use of rewards is about understanding what makes your dog tick. Utilizing only a few of these options limits your ability to effectively reinforce desirable behaviors, because these will vary in degree of difficulty in various environments.

Reinforcement Hierarchy

Individual preferences, experience, and context will influence the value of any reward. For example, in the initial stages of their relationship with their family, most dogs perceive praise as minimum wage. On the other hand, special food treats are viewed more like winning a jackpot or receiving a bonus at work.

Make a list in rank order of the most to least desirable rewards for your dog. What would your dog add to the list if he was given free choice of everything he comes across? This would likely include much more than simply toys and treats. This list will help you determine when to employ specific rewards.

When selecting rewards for a particular situation, keep in mind that they will

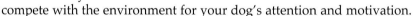

compete with the environment for your dog's attention and motivation.

Also consider the amount of motivation he will need to accomplish a particular task or request. For example, if you are trying to train your dog in an environment like an outdoor group training class, the rate and value of reinforcement should be high enough to compete with the many distractions in that environment.

TRAINING TRUTH

Self-Reinforcing Behaviors

Certain canine behaviors are reinforcing in and of themselves. They require no outside encouragement, such as offering a reward. Some of these include exploration, investigation, digging, play, jumping, and barking. To effectively maintain your dog's focus, you must offer him rewards that are more powerful than these self-reinforcing behaviors. Effective rewards for your dog can vary from day to day, or even moment to moment. His reaction depends on what he has access to at a particular time, and your dog may find some of these things to be of equal or greater value. Be prepared to adjust what, when, and how you give rewards to maintain your dog's motivation to actively participate in the training game.

Reward Options

Food Rewards

For many dogs, food is one of the most powerful motivators and therefore one of the most useful rewards at your disposal. Because so many food rewards are perceived as being of high value by so many dogs, they are most useful when teaching new behaviors or working in new environments. Over time, rewards can be used more variably to maintain established behaviors. Ideally, your dog's daily intake of food should be broken into two parts.

1. Food offered from hollow chew toys at mealtimes:
   Feeding your dog his core meals from hollow toys is much more productive than feeding him from a bowl. It provides non-aerobic mental and physical exercise. This keeps him busy doing something acceptable, which prevents unwanted behavior.
2. Food offered as reinforcements in planned training sessions and as a reward for appropriate behavior throughout the day:
   Tiny food rewards are like deposits in the bank of good behavior or data into your dog's memory drive each time they are used to teach or maintain desired behaviors.
   Food rewards can be used for multiple repetitions, even in a brief training session.

Have a range of low-, medium-, and high-value rewards on hand for your dog. Use the highest value foods for more challenging training situations and the lowest for the least challenging. Choose healthy treats that also have nutritional value in addition to their use to leverage desirable behavior.

Food rewards should be used most when teaching new behaviors and when working in a new, more challenging environment. They are easily dispensed and quickly consumed, which makes it easy to encourage repetition of the desired behavior. As your dog's training progresses, begin to incorporate other types of rewards. This ensures that you have access to a variety of behavior-strengthening tools.

Praise and Petting with a Purpose

Praise and petting are two useful rewards that are always at your disposal. They can be offered even when your dog is at a distance. Their main purpose is to provide feedback to your dog about his presence and behavior.

The act of petting a dog also triggers the release of endorphins, which can have a calming effect on both the dog and the person.

However, praise and petting can also have the opposite effect on some dogs. They become too aroused and cannot focus on the task at hand. Enthusiastically petting a dog that is already highly aroused will intensify his state of mind. As you become familiar with your dog's preferences and tolerance for specific situations, you can better gauge when and where to use praise as a reward. Some owners also find it challenging to offer praise and petting at precisely the right moment to reinforce desired behavior.

Praise Problems

Praise is essential to your relationship with your dog. But, it is sometimes offered in a way that has the opposite effect of what was intended, which is to strengthen behaviors you want.

Timing

Offering praise before or too long after a behavior is ineffective. However, it can be difficult to use your voice to pinpoint precisely when you are pleased with your dog's behavior. For example, your dog *sits* and you start praising him. He then jumps up, but it takes a few seconds before you stop praising. Meanwhile, he has been praised for sitting *and* jumping up. In this case, a marker, such as a clicker or the word *"yes,"* is useful to accurately pinpoint the desired behavior.

DANGER!

One of the most common training errors is poorly timed reinforcements. This can result in inadvertently rewarding the dog for unwanted behaviors. For example, when a dog jumps on its owner, many people respond by looking at the dog, saying *"Get down,"* and pushing him off. In reality, the dog has been potentially rewarded in this scenario three times: when the owner looked at the dog, talked to the dog, and touched the dog. For most dogs, any attention—even negative—is better than being ignored.

Intensity

The manner in which you offer praise also affects your dog, sometimes negatively. The intensity of praise should be geared toward your dog's temperament and level of training, as well as the situation. Overly exuberant praise may overstimulate your dog and temporarily inhibit his ability to learn. Some dogs become so excited by praise that they may urinate in response.

On the other hand, praise may not be an effective reward if it is not sufficiently enthusiastic. Some dogs are naturally calm and relaxed, and they need a real pep talk to motivate them. You may also need to ramp it up when your dog is distracted by something he sees as a more valuable reward. If you find it difficult to praise exuberantly or tone down your praise so that you don't overstimulate your dog, you should use other forms of rewards.

Let's Get Physical

Physical contact, like a pat on the head, is not necessarily reward-ing for every dog. If it is com-bined with praise, it may be too exciting for a dog that has not yet learned self-control. In general, calmly, gently rubbing or scratch-ing your dog on the chest is a good option.

PAWS TO CONSIDER

Some of your most valuable training tools are a positive attitude and realistic expecta-tions. Training does not always progress smoothly or quickly. But, these tools invariably make the learning process more enjoy-able for both you and your dog.

Play

Play enhances your relationship with your dog and brings joy to your day. When choosing games, make sure they are appropriate for your dog's tem-perament, the particular environment, and your training goals. For example, some dogs can play tugging games in a mannerly fashion. Others find it far too stimulating.

If your dog enjoys a particular game and you are confident that he can play by rules that reinforce mannerly, safe behavior, then go for it. But think twice if a particular game causes your dog to growl, refuse to surrender objects, or become too excited to respond reliably to requests. You may want to forgo these games until you have had time to work on these behaviors in brief, controlled sessions.

In general, most play should be initiated and terminated by you. This ensures that your dog understands that you control access to the fun. You can remind your dog of this rule by asking him to respond to requests before and many times during play.

Life Rewards

Preferred activities can also be used as rewards to reinforce desired behavior. Favorite canine activities include heading out the door for a walk, entering a dog run, being invited on the couch for a snuggle, or being given permis-sion to enjoy an extra long sniff on a walk. These and others can be used to reinforce potentially less preferred activities such as sitting

at the door or dog run gate, or walking on a loose leash.

Toy Story

Toys are crucial for recreation, therapy, to relieve boredom and stress, and to prevent inappropriate behaviors. Without an interesting toy or two, a dog will always find something to occupy his time. He may play with something you consider valuable or pass the time by barking incessantly.

Dog toys have moved beyond basic squeaky toys and balls. Modern dog toys are designed to stimulate your dog's brain and encourage the development of appropriate behaviors.

Many owners make the mistake of purchasing toys that they find appealing. Your choices should be based on safety and your dog's preferences. Observing your dog playing with toys tells you everything you need to know about his preferences.

Dogs often find new toys more interesting and can become bored with old, familiar toys. You can maintain your dog's enthusiasm for toys by offering them to him on a rotating basis. An old toy he hasn't had access to in a week will surely be cause for a minor celebration. You can also increase your dog's enthusiasm for toys by incorporating them in play and hiding them in easy-to-find spots and then celebrating with him when he makes a discovery.

Stuffable Chew Toys: Brain Training for Dogs

Food-stuffable, puzzle, or enrichment toys are the most valuable items you can add to your dog's toy treasure chest. They come in many shapes, sizes, and colors, but all function in a similar manner and serve a similar purpose. They are hollow in the middle and designed to hold food. Extracting it requires varying degrees of effort by your dog. Some can be filled with dry, pellet-type food, some with wet food, and others with both. Getting it out requires the dog to chew, lick, and push the toy around with his paws and nose.

There are two general types of food-stuffable toys:
1. Those that hold and dispense food a bit at a time when the dog pushes the toy with his nose or paws.
2. Those that hold food that is not dispensed but will keep your dog busy trying to get at it (like marrow in a real bone).

Dogs are genetically programmed to hunt for their food. Normally, this activity requires an enormous amount of physical and mental energy. For pet dogs, this time- and energy-consuming activity is replaced by food presented in a dish at predictable times.

Start with toys that have larger openings so the food easily falls out with a push of the paw or nose. Then try adding bigger pieces of food that require a more concerted effort to extract. Some toys have adjustable openings so you can use the same size food and simply modify the toy. You can also hide toys around the house so your dog has to hunt for them prior to unpacking them.

Other Types of Toys

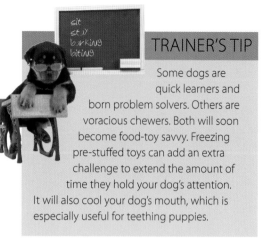

Digestible Chew Toys

Some chew toys are designed for safe digestion. They have a relatively brief lifespan, and your dog should have only a limited number of them each week. Supervise your dog whenever he plays with a digestible chew toy because even these can be broken into pieces that can be caught in his throat.

Plush, Squeaker Toys

Plush toys seem to be the go-to choice for many pet parents (probably because some of them are so darn cute), and many dogs are certainly fans. These toys can play a valuable role in a dog's daily routine as rewards. They can also be used for interactive and cooperative play with family members in games like fetch. It is generally best to reserve them for supervised and interactive play, as some dogs can chew through the lining and possibly ingest the filling or squeaker.

Some trainers recommend avoiding plush toys altogether for fear that they will elicit prey drive or aggressive behavior. However, there is no real basis for this concern as long as you have instilled a foundation of socialization and cooperation to ensure that your dog will relinquish toys on request (see the Object Exchange exercise on page 110 and anti–resource guarding exercises on page 189).

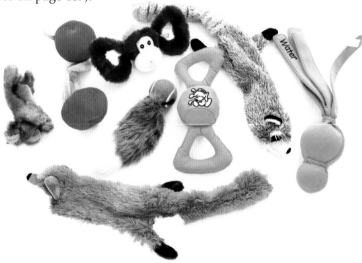

Rope Toys

Rope toys can be ideal for games of tug. However, they closely resemble household items (such as carpet fringe) and may confuse your dog and lead to inappropriate chewing. Further, if you choose to play tug with your dog, you must be confident that he will release the tug object on cue (see page 191 for another Object Exchange exercise).

Timing and Ratio of Rewards

Continuous Reinforcement

When every occurrence of a behavior earns a reward, it is called continuous reinforcement. In the initial stages of teaching, this can be a useful reward ratio (i.e., one behavior results in one reward) to strengthen the behavior.

CHECKLIST

Benefits of Food-Stuffable Toys:

Food-dispensing toys provide enrichment by utilizing the instinctive canine desire to find food in the environment. This time-consuming activity of unpacking food stuffed into toys keeps your dog occupied and helps to prevent unwanted behaviors, such as excessive barking and inappropriate chewing.

✓ They provide an outlet for your dog's physical and mental energy.

✓ They can help prevent countless inappropriate behaviors. A busy dog is not making up his own entertainment, such as refashioning your slippers.

✓ Chewing on safe toys can help keep your dog's gums and teeth in good health.

✓ They make crate time fun!

✓ They fulfill your dog's instinctual desire to hunt for food. Giving food away in a bowl provides no outlet for this instinct.

✓ Providing your dog with chew/puzzle toys on your departure keeps him busy and can help prevent the development of separation issues.

✓ They can help alleviate guilt you might have when you are unable to spend time with your dog.

Generally, when you are teaching a new behavior, you should provide a high-value reward for every correct response. However, as your dog develops proficiency at a task in a specific setting, you can gradually vary the rate and value of the rewards. Make sure to be more generous and offer higher value rewards whenever you ask your dog to do something especially challenging, such as coming when called in a park with lots of distractions.

Decreasing the ratio or value of reinforcements too quickly can weaken established behaviors. Do not assume that your dog reliably understands what is expected until he has a strong history of practice and reinforcements. Just like building physical muscles, learning muscles require many repetitions to strengthen.

Variable Reinforcement

Turn Your Dog into a Gambler Part of the art of dog training is to keep your dog guessing about when and how he will be rewarded. Slot machines are a great example of the power of variable reinforcement. In this case, putting a coin in the slot and pulling a lever again and again indicates the hopes of the occasional reward. Variable reinforcement usually produces a stable and high rate of correct responses that dogs rarely forget. As your dog masters a new lesson, rewards should also be offered variably to maintain established behaviors. Over time, the reward schedule can also be adjusted so that you can get more behaviors for fewer rewards. For example, you might ask your dog for a *down*, then a *sit*, then a *paw wave* to earn the toss of a toy.

TRAINING TRUTH

Toy Safety

Safety is a paramount concern when choosing toys. No dog toy is completely indestructible, but some are certainly more durable, safe, and economical, because you won't need to constantly replace them.

Toys fall into two general categories:
• Toys that your dog can safely play with unsupervised
• Toys that he should have only under supervision

Make sure to consider the following when choosing toys:
• Assess your dog's chewing strength and enthusiasm when selecting appropriate toys.
• Avoid toys that are small enough to fit entirely into your dog's mouth, as well as anything with small parts that might be ingested.
• Supervise your dog when he first tries out a new toy so you can assess its durability.
• Be cautious of rawhide, which is not highly digestible and can be difficult for some dogs to break down into safely consumable bits.
• Avoid purchasing plush toys that closely resemble household items or furnishings.

Thoroughly clean stuffable toys prior to each use.

Let your dog see you as a slot machine that is fun to play. Just be sure your payouts are better than the rewards they are likely to find on their own in the environment.

Delivery of Rewards

Your method of delivering rewards will also impact your dog's motivation to offer another desired behavior. To begin, potential rewards should be shown up front. Later on, they can be hidden and offered immediately after a behavior is performed.

Use your treat delivery to set up the next repetition, which varies from behavior to behavior. For example, for a *sit* or *down*, toss the treat a foot or so away so your dog must get up and then come back to try again. When working on *stay*, consider delivering the reward while the dog is in position. When working on walking nicely on leash, offer the reward while the dog is in the desired heeling position.

Markers

Effective communication is a key component to successfully teaching our dogs. A marker is one of the most useful tools for establishing a clear dialogue for communication. A marker is a sound that is paired with a reward so that your dog makes a connection between the two. This allows you to pinpoint a particular action your dog was engaged in. For example, if you want your dog to sit, you would use the marker right as his rear makes contact with the ground and follow that with a reward. The marker is like taking a perfectly focused picture of a behavior so that your dog has the best chance of knowing precisely what it is you want—doing so results in your dog trying a repetition of the behavior to create a repetition of the reward. Think of the marker like a slot machine ringing loudly. You don't need to see money pouring out of the machine to know that good stuff is on the way!

The marker becomes a sort of contract with your dog, and the following are the terms of the contract:
- A reward will immediately follow the mark. Even if you clicked or said the verbal marker at the "wrong" moment, you must reward your dog or he will lose trust in the marker sound.
- Once the mark happens, it also signals the end of the required behavior. You are essentially releasing your dog until the next repetition or request.

- However, a marker is not a cue or request for a behavior. It is part of a reward system. It allows you to offer precise feedback and pinpoint specific moments to give your dog a clear image of what you want. If you click or say *"Yes"* the moment your dog's nose

DANGER!

Do not hold the clicker close to your dog's ear. If you put it close to your own and click it, you'll find the sound is not pleasant.

touches your hand and then give him a reward after a number of repetitions, he will realize that his nose touching your palm was the action that earned the treat.

Choosing a Marker

A marker can be a word or a sound made with a clicker, which is a small, handheld device that makes a clicking sound when a small button is pressed.

A clicker is useful because our physical reflexes (pressing the clicker) are usually faster than our voice. The click is also a unique sound that has no possible negative connections for the dog. But, some sound-sensitive dogs may be initially startled by it, in which case you should muffle the sound by holding the clicker in your shirtsleeve or pocket.

You can also choose a word as a marker. The benefit of a verbal marker instead of or in addition to a clicker is that your voice is readily accessible. The purpose of a marker is to offer precise feedback to your dog. Choose a short distinctive word. *"Yes!"* may be preferable to *"Good,"* which is a word we tend to toss around more frequently.

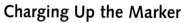

Charging Up the Marker

When introducing your dog to the marker, you can jump right in and use it to mark a specific behavior, so the dog doesn't get any noncontingent marks and treats. For example, wait for your dog to *sit*, then mark and reward.

Alternatively, you can begin with a brief marker-charging session. This may benefit your dog and provide you with an opportunity to become comfortable using the clicker or marker word and timing the sequence of behavior, mark, treat.

With a bowl of treats at easy reach, hold the clicker behind your back (so you don't inadvertently push it at the dog's face and so the sound is a bit muffled), and proceed with the following.

- Make the marker sound.
- Give a treat.
- Repeat several times and be sure that your dog receives one treat for each mark.

After several repetitions, check to see if your dog understands that the marker means a reward is forthcoming. Make the sound and observe his response. When you click or say "*Yes*," he should whip around and look at you. If not, repeat the exercise a few more times.

As soon as your dog makes this connection, you can use the marker as a training tool to accurately pinpoint desired behaviors.

Release Word

A release word indicates that the exercise is over and your dog is on "free time." When using a marker to instill behaviors, the marker indicates your dog has completed the required behavior for the reward, and the exercise is finished. If you want your dog to continue the exercise—for example, staying in position—then delay the marker. Additionally, you can also use a release word to let your dog know when he is finished and on "free time." This is particularly important when you fade the use of the marker.

Other Valuable Tools

Reinforcement of Incompatible Behaviors

It's much easier and more pleasant to show your dog what you *want* him to do than punishing him for what you *don't* want. An example of this is teaching a new behavior that can be used to replace an unwanted habit. The frequency of an undesirable behavior can be decreased by reinforcing (or strengthening) a competing behavior. For instance, teach your dog to *sit* on cue, and ask him to do this when greeting people rather than jumping on them. Other examples include teaching your dog to *come when called* to replace chasing the cat, or teaching him to *lie down* on his bed rather than beg at the table.

Reward Removal

Behaviors are sustained through rewards. Temporarily barring your dog's access to rewards can be an exceptionally effective way to teach him that certain behaviors are not rewarding. For example, if your dog jumps up to grab a treat from your hand, raise your hand out of his reach until he stops jumping. This will help him learn to take food politely (with four feet on the floor).

This is an easy, effective, and nonconfrontational approach. Just be sure you are skilled at identifying the things that your dog considers reward-ing in a particular context. This is not always obvious to the untrained eye. For instance, simply making eye con-tact is a reward from the dog's point of view. This is something that many own-ers don't realize.

Some owners reward their dog unintentionally by looking at him while he is engaged in an undesirable behavior, such as jumping up.

Punishments

A punishment is any event that is painful, damaging, or uncomfortable and reduces the probability that a specific behavior will be repeated. It can be something the dog doesn't like, known as positive punishment. It can also be accomplished by removing something the dog likes, known as negative punishment. Either way, a punishment is an unpleasant experience. Keep in mind that punishment may teach the dog to stop doing something, how-ever, it will not teach him *what* you would like him to do instead. Therefore, your dog may simply switch to another behavior you consider equally inappropriate.

Another drawback is that if you continually berate your dog, he will begin to tune you out, requiring you to yell louder and longer each time. In the long run, it is far more productive to teach your dog appropriate behaviors that decrease the likelihood of his engaging in unwanted behaviors.

Punishment can also have unwanted consequences, such as triggering stress, fear, and aggression. For example, yanking on a leash when a dog attempts to enthusiastically greet someone may cause the dog to become apprehensive around people because he will learn to associate this with pain.

In addition, your dog may decide that punishment is contingent on the presence of the person administering the punishing. For example, reprimanding your dog for eliminating on the carpet may be motivated by a desire to stop him from having accidents in the house. But, he may get the idea that it is never okay to eliminate in front of people, even when you take him for a walk to relieve himself.

Unfortunately, punishment is often strongly reinforcing for the punisher, and this makes him or her likely to continue punishing rather than focusing on a more positive approach, such as teaching a dog what is expected. This can result in a dog who comes to view life with humans as stressful and scary.

Cues/Requests/Commands

Just as the word "leader" has some potentially negative connotations, the word "command" is likewise associated with a less progressive approach to teaching our canine companions. It sounds like a bit of an implied threat. Technically, a more correct term is "cue."

You'll notice that throughout this book, both "cue" and "request" will be used. A "cue" or "request" is an opportunity to do something in order to earn a reward.

Impulse Control

Impulse control is the ability to control a behavior in order to achieve delayed gratification.

Systematic Desensitization

This is a gradual process to familiarize a dog with something that is potentially frightening. At first, the dog has very limited exposure to the stimulus.

As the dog becomes accustomed to its proximity, this exposure is gradually increased. Eventually, the dog will become comfortable in the presence of this stimulus.

Habituation

Habituation is the process of helping your dog become accustomed to a stimulus so he is less likely to be fearful or overly excited when exposed to it. Unlike systematic desensitization, there is no effort to increase the intensity of the stimulus.

Classical Conditioning

Classical conditioning creates an association between a stimulus (person, place, or thing) and something that has positive significance to your dog. This works very well in conjunction with systematic desensitization. For example, if a dog is afraid of men wearing hats, classical conditioning can be used to help him overcome this problem. This could be accomplished by repetitively giving him high-value food treats while a man wearing a hat walks by. The dog will eventually make a positive association between the valued resource (food treats) and the presence of a man wearing a hat.

Counterconditioning

Otherwise known as changing your dog's opinion of a person, place, or thing, counterconditioning helps your dog establish a new opinion of something (a person, place, or thing) by pairing it with something he values (a reward). For the process to work you must offer a very high value reward to ensure that it will override the dog's previous negative association.

Generalization

This is the process of teaching your dog to respond reliably in a variety of situations and to respond positively to people. Teaching a new behavior is best done in an environment that is calm and free of distractions. But, it's also important to gradually introduce distractions so your dog learns to use his skills in a variety of situations and environments. When working toward generalization, increase the distractions gradually as your dog develops more ability to focus and ignore them.

Shaping

Shaping is the reinforcement of successive approximations toward a desired behavior. The goal is to gradually refine your dog's response toward the desired behavior. For example, if you are teaching your dog to step up on a stool, you might begin by reinforcing the action of simply looking in the direction of the stool. When he does this reliably, you would begin reinforcing the action of stepping toward the stool. As training progresses, the behaviors that are reinforced gradually come closer to the desired behavior.

Throwing Behaviors

Some dogs experiment with a number of behaviors when trying to elicit a rewarding response from their trainer. They might sit and then lie down, spin, or bark. This can be a cute routine, but most people prefer their dog to more often offer behaviors in response to cues or requests.

Environmental Enrichment

The typical pet dog's environment is relatively boring. Most spend their day at home while their family is out. The routine is broken up only by brief potty breaks during the week, and some longer walks or activities on weekends. Your dog's development and overall well-being are strongly affected by the stimulation (or lack thereof) in his environment. Make an effort to provide your dog with a more interesting environment at home. This can be as simple as hiding food-stuffed chew toys for him to find, or regularly changing your route for his daily walk. Impromptu training sessions also provide mental challenges for him. Plan brief repetitions of your dog's lessons throughout the day, provide mental and physical diversion, and improve his training skills. Just like physical muscles, learning muscles grow stronger through repetition and need to be maintained.

Training Equipment

Treat Pouch
A treat pouch attached to your hip may not put you on any "best-dressed" fashion lists, but this is a very handy way to have rewards available to reinforce good behavior the moment it happens. Missing these opportunities will slow down your dog's rate of learning.

Leash
A sturdy leather or nylon leash of approximately 6 feet (1.8 meters) is essential for safe walks. A shorter leash—4 to 6 feet (1.2 to 1.8 meters) should be used for an indoor tether.

Extendable or Retractable Leashes
These leads extend out 15 feet (4.6 meters) or more, giving your dog a broader range of freedom on leash. They can be useful when working on distance exercises outdoors. However, they are generally regarded as unnecessary. They can also pose a safety hazard if you do not

have full control of the brake/locking mechanism. If your dog ranges out of your view, you may not have time to intervene if he confronts a hazard like a menacing dog or speeding car. The thin nylon can also be difficult to see and may trip or entangle people and other dogs. Another drawback is that the constant tension on these types of leashes encourages dogs to pull rather than walk at your side.

Tethers

A leash of or nylon-coated cable approximately 4 feet (1.2 meters) in length with sturdy snaps at both ends should be used to temporarily restrain your dog in your presence. The tether is useful to instill polite greetings; for quiet, self-pacifying time with a chew toy; as a time-out; or as an aid in housetraining. A tether can be used everywhere in your home where you regularly spend time with your dog.

Harnesses

By definition, harnesses were designed to efficiently utilize an animal's weight-pulling ability by distributing the weight across broad straps around the torso and back—hence the use of harnesses for sled dogs, carriage horses, and other freight animals. Of course, they are also used to walk dogs, and they produce the same result of making it easier and more comfortable for a dog to pull hard. Harnesses are generally not recommended for teaching a dog to walk nicely on leash.

The exception is the front-clip harness, where the leash is connected to a metal ring on the front of the chest strap. This design works on a different principle than traditional harnesses that position the leash ring on the dog's back.

Front-clip harnesses can be very useful and effective to curb pulling because they limit the dog's forward momentum rather than encouraging his pulling reflex. This can be a useful management tool when teaching your dog to walk nicely by your side.

Head Halters

Similar to halters used for horses, head halters control your dog's head, which makes it easier to control the rest of his body. One strap circles around the dog's muzzle, and the other circles around his neck.

This training tool causes intense alarm for many pet parents because it closely resembles a muzzle. However, head halters are not muzzles. They do not inhibit the dog's ability to open his mouth. They inhibit his ability to pull.

Dogs should be introduced to a head halter gradually. Some require a few days to acclimate to it and may paw at it, jump, or be reluctant to move forward while wearing it.

- For a couple of days, present the head halter at your dog's mealtimes. Feed him through the nose loop of the halter by holding it in front of his muzzle with one hand, and holding a piece of food on the other side. The dog must insert his nose through the loop to get to the food. Gradually increase the distance he must move to put his nose into the loop.
- Begin increasing the duration of time that his nose is inserted into the halter by offering a few more pieces of food.
- When your dog seems comfortable eating with the loop over his muzzle, loosely place the straps over the back of his neck while offering food.

When used gently and properly, head halters are humane and effective. However, you should avoid harshly jerking the leash, or using a head halter with a retractable leash. The force of running to the end of a retractable line and being jerked back abruptly can cause injury.

Also, check for possible irritation if the halter strap rubs against his muzzle. Some brands are designed with nosebands similar to those on horse halters. You can also create your own by lining the halter with moleskin.

Collars
Invest in a sturdy plain buckle collar with an identification tag or plate attached.

Martingale/Limited Slip Collar
This style of collar is a good choice for safety. If the dog pulls, it tightens and remains securely on the dog, but it does not tighten enough to choke. This is a good choice for dogs with narrow heads because they cannot back out, which can happen with a normal buckle collar.

Choke/Slip Collars
Made of nylon or metal chain, these collars tighten when the ring attached to the leash is pulled. As with most things, the choke collar has pros and cons. However, the list of pros is short. It is a safe collar design for walks because the dog can't back out of it. On the other hand, the list of cons for this tool is long and deserves serious consideration. Choking a dog is not only completely unnecessary and unkind, but it is also likely to aggravate the dog and increase frustration. Plus, most dogs eventually become impervious to the choking sensation of these collars and continue to drag their owners down the street, coughing and hacking all the way.

Prong/Spike Collars

These collars are made up of interlocking metal or plastic links, each with two prongs. When tightened, the prongs pinch the skin and exert pressure on the dog's neck. Like choke collars, prong collars are generally not recommended. They can aggravate the dog and escalate arousal, excitement, and frustration, as well as trigger aggression on walks. Pinching and poking a dog with prongs is not likely to encourage a calm, cooperative state of mind. These collars also pose a safety risk because the prongs may bend and loosen, causing the collar to drop off the dog's neck.

Shock Collars

These collars transmit an electrical shock that is intended to interrupt the dog's behavior. In a nutshell, electric or shock collars are to be avoided at all costs. They often create serious side effects that are far worse than the issue for which they were employed and may cause intense pain and stress to your dog. If you find it challenging to keep your dog under control through management and gentle training, you should employ the assistance of a professional trainer rather than a shock collar.

Bowls

A stainless steel water bowl (which is easier to keep clean and free from bacteria) is a necessity. However, a food bowl is an option, because feeding from food-stuffable toys is ideal for mental and physical exercise.

Dog Bed

While dogs are masters at finding all sorts of comfy spots to lounge and snuggle, a plush dog bed is a useful tool for training your dog to use a go-to spot while you eat or entertain visitors.

Housetraining

ousetraining is a fundamental component of every companion dog's life skills. Life with a house trained dog is far easier for you, as there is no need for constant cleanups. It's also much less stressful for your dog, as he is less apt to suffer from being reprimanded. From a dog's perspective, it doesn't get much worse than happily greeting his family's arrival, and in turn receiving a harsh scolding when they discover a puddle or pile.

Dogs have a natural inclination for cleanliness, which makes them highly receptive to learning elimination patterns. When they are three or four weeks old, puppies are able to move around and eliminate on their own. They will instinctively choose to do this away from their sleeping quarters and move away from the soiled area. Reinforcing this natural tendency toward cleanliness is at the core of good housetraining skills. This makes it easy to set your dog up for housetraining success by tailoring training to his natural tendencies. The most effective way to accomplish this is by utilizing management tools, which will help you recognize your dog's elimination patterns.

Housetraining Defined

Teaching your dog when and where you want him to eliminate is what housetraining is all about. For some dogs, this will be exclusively outdoors. Other dogs are trained to go outdoors sometimes, and to also use an indoor potty system, such as pads, paper, or a litter box. In some cases, small dogs are trained exclusively to use an indoor system.

House training is an all-or-nothing proposition, which requires an honest evaluation of your dog's level of training. If you find yourself saying "Yes, he is housetrained, but he sometimes makes mistakes," your dog isn't really housetrained. A clear definition of housetraining is the first step in the training process.

The Magic of Management

Managing your dog's time enables you to most accurately predict when he needs to eliminate. This is the key to housetraining success. If you know when he needs to go, you only need to take him to the right spot and reward him when he relieves himself. Accidents happen when your dog is in the wrong place at the right time, running loose in

PAWS TO CONSIDER

An indoor potty area can offer a degree of convenience, especially if you own a small dog and live in an apartment building. However, it's a good idea to teach even tiny dogs to also eliminate outdoors. Daily walks are a physically and mentally enriching part of every dog's routine.

your home when he needs to eliminate. He can also be in the right place at the wrong time, such as out for a walk when he does not need to go. Sooner or later, he will need to go after you have arrived back home.

Management tools help you get your dog to the designated toilet area at the appropriate time. Dogs learn to eliminate exclusively in one designated

area by repeating the behavior and consistently being rewarded for it. Rewards will help your dog develop a strong preference for this pattern. Once he forms a habit, your dog will be far less inclined to consider eliminating anywhere else. However, this doesn't happen because he wants to abide by human standards. It happens because you have successfully instilled a desirable elimination behavior pattern, and deviating from this makes him uncomfortable. This is a housetrained dog.

As a rule of thumb, dogs need to eliminate after waking up, after play or a period of excitement, and approximately a half hour to an hour after eating or drinking. In general, younger, more active dogs

DANGER!

Lax Housetraining

Owners generally don't mind cleaning up a puppy's housetraining accidents. But, this level of tolerance is usually temporary, even for a very small dog. As your dog matures, poor housetraining skills are less likely to be forgiven and forgotten. This is one of the main reasons why otherwise lovely dogs are surrendered to shelters every day.

Poorly housetrained dogs are often banished to the backyard or basement by their families. In this situation, they have no chance of becoming housetrained, and they are likely to develop additional behavior problems, such as excessive barking, destructive behavior, and digging due to loneliness, stress, and boredom. Dogs are social creatures, which is why they make such wonderful companions. Prolonged and excessive social banishment resulting from lack of housetraining skills—or for any other reason—is especially cruel for canine companions.

eliminate more frequently. As your puppy matures and you adhere to a time management strategy, he will develop stronger bladder and bowel muscle control. You will gradually be able to increase the length of time you expect him to "hold it."

Regardless of your dog's age, personality, experience, or activity level, the following management tools will help you accurately predict when he needs to eliminate:

- Chew toys
- On-leash supervision
- Short-term confinement
- Long-term confinement
- A feeding, watering, and walking schedule

These management tools will also help to prevent and manage many other behaviors including excessive barking, play nipping, counter surfing, chewing inappropriate items, inappropriate greetings, and separation issues.

How Long Does Housetraining Take?

Keep in mind that every dog is an individual. Dogs progress at different rates when learning new skills, including housetraining. Your dog's age, temperament, activity level, health, and previous experiences will influence his learning curve. But, the most important factor is your ability to help him succeed. Consider all of these factors as you plan a strategy to use the management tools at your disposal, and do not overestimate your dog's ability to understand and respond to your lessons.

Most dogs start to understand a housetraining routine after a few weeks of reinforcing the pattern. However, you should plan for a full year of careful management to ensure that your dog is fully housetrained. This may seem excessive, but gradual progress is the best route to long-term success.

TRAINING TRUTH

Are Some Dogs Easier to Housetrain than Others?

Generalized misperceptions about age, breed, or type are often used to explain inadequate housetraining.

The fact that one Golden Retriever was reliably housetrained at five months of age does not mean all Golden Retrievers will follow suit. Every dog is an individual. Within any breed, type, or litter of pups, there will be a huge range of personalities. Some dogs learn very quickly and are particular about keeping themselves and their sleeping areas clean. Others require more time and careful management to learn a housetraining routine.

It may take longer to housetrain a tiny dog, but this is not because the dog has a small bladder. It is because owners tend to be far more tolerant of a tiny dog's housetraining mishaps, and therefore less likely to utilize management tools that will set the dog on course for housetraining success.

A year of consistent reinforcement ensures that the habit is well established. On the other hand, if you rush things, you may end up with a two-year-old dog that still has accidents in the house. Housetraining should not be seen as a race to the finish line.

Dedication to Training

By far, the most important factor is an owner's commitment to reinforcing the routine. For instance, a smart, fastidious pup may want to keep his sleeping area clean. But, he won't be successful unless his family provides adequate walks; careful supervision during playtime in the house; and a well-planned feeding, watering, and walking schedule. Regardless of your dog's breed or age, his housetraining success is ultimately your responsibility.

Gender Issues

Another common misperception is the idea that one or the other gender is easier to housetrain. In reality, it doesn't really matter. Both male and female dogs can be successfully housetrained. Individuals of both sexes may also need extra assistance to achieve housetraining success.

Age Matters—Sometimes

It is often easier to housetrain an adult dog than a puppy because most adult dogs have stronger bladder and bowel muscle control than very young pups. Some dogs have remarkable control. They can "hold it" for twelve or more hours. However, it is unfair to expect this from any dog. Aside from being unkind, this excessive strain on their kidneys could result in health issues. In general, adult dogs should have opportunities to eliminate at least every seven to eight hours. For puppies, this number is greatly decreased.

However, if an adult dog has been consistently permitted to have accidents in the house, this behavior is probably strongly ingrained. It will require diligent effort to help a dog overcome this pattern and replace it with a new, stronger habit of eliminating in the right spot.

Regardless of the dog's age, the general approach to housetraining success is the same. It is the rate of progress and the degree to which management tools are used that will vary.

Additional Considerations

Unpredictable factors can also prolong or complicate the process. Dogs are creatures of habit, and they can have trouble adjusting to changes in their environment and routine. The stress of a new housemate, visitor, or tension in the home can trigger housetraining mistakes. Even a reliably trained dog can have accidents in these situations. The best remedy is to stabilize your dog's environment and review your management techniques to prevent additional mistakes.

Designing a Housetraining Routine

Pick a Potty Spot

Decide where you want your dog's toilet area to be from day one so you can begin to establish good housetraining habits right away. When choosing an appropriate toilet area for your dog, consider his size, age, and home environment, as well as your household schedule. For most medium- or large-sized dogs the goal is training them to eliminate exclusively outdoors. However, many people use a temporary indoor potty area for young pups because they need to eliminate so frequently. When the dog is four or five months old, you should curtail his access to this indoor area if you don't want this to become a permanent part of his routine. A small dog can be taught to eliminate both outdoors and indoors on pads, paper, or in a specially designed indoor potty box.

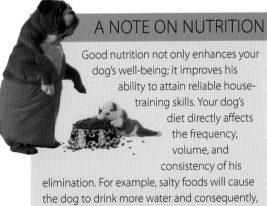

A NOTE ON NUTRITION

Good nutrition not only enhances your dog's well-being; it improves his ability to attain reliable housetraining skills. Your dog's diet directly affects the frequency, volume, and consistency of his elimination. For example, salty foods will cause the dog to drink more water and consequently, he will need to urinate more frequently. Talk to your veterinarian if you suspect that your dog's diet is contributing to housetraining problems.

Training your pup to eliminate on a variety of surfaces—concrete, grass, gravel, and dirt—is ideal, since you never know what sort of surfaces will be available, especially when traveling.

If you want your dog to eliminate on the street, consider both etiquette and ease. Choose an area that is easily accessible but not likely to create a nuisance for passersby. Use the leash to gently guide your dog off the main walk area to prevent him from soiling directly where people walk.

If you have a safely enclosed yard, you probably consider it a prized location for hanging out with your dog, friends, and family. Therefore, it's a good idea to teach your dog to eliminate in one designated area of the yard so it's easy to keep the area as clean as possible. Provide your dog with a suitably sized, special potty area in the yard, and teach him to eliminate in this spot. During the housetraining process, your yard should be treated like a room inside your house. Take him to the appropriate spot on leash and reward him for eliminating there. Give him some freedom in the house and yard only after he is reliably trained to eliminate only in the designated toilet area.

High-Rise Housetraining

For most dogs in a suburban or rural environment, housetraining is a one-step process of learning to eliminate outdoors. But for most city pups, this is a two-step process. They are first taught to eliminate indoors on pads or

in a litter box, and then they are taught to eliminate outdoors. Puppies need to eliminate frequently, and it may be unrealistic to get a pup into an elevator and down to the sidewalk as frequently as necessary.

It's also challenging for a young puppy to "hold it" while making the journey from the apartment through a hallway, down an elevator, and out the lobby. If your dog is small enough, carry him outside. If not, lure him with a food-stuffed toy held at nose level to get out the door. Also, be sure to have everything you need for potty breaks easily accessible (cleanup bags, treat pouch, and coat).

Chew Toys: Keeping Your Dog Busy Doing the Right Thing

Playing with chew toys is an essential daily activity for your dog. Their value increases exponentially when combined with other management tools, such as on-leash tethering and crate training. Giving your dog a couple of chew toys when employing other tools will keep him happily and safely occupied and will prevent housetraining mistakes.

On-Leash Supervision and Tethering

Keeping your dog on a 6-foot (1.8-meter) leash when you can supervise him is a simple and effective way to prevent housetraining mistakes. If your dog is by your side or tethered nearby, playing with you or his toys, you can monitor his behavior. This is no different than carefully supervising a two-year-old child in your home, but you can't hold your dog's paw like you can hold a child's hand. The leash provides a gentle, effective way to control and manage your pup.

Tethering can also be used as a time-out to stop play nipping, jumping on people or counters, or other inappropriate behaviors (see information on time-outs on page 48).

On-leash supervision and tethering also allows your dog to become accustomed to different areas of your home in a safe, controlled manner. It is especially useful when managing supervised introductions between dogs and children (see Chapter Six on page 111). On-leash supervision and

PAWS TO CONSIDER

Killing with Kindness

You may worry that your dog will be overly restricted if he is confined to a crate or wears a leash indoors, but it takes only a few moments for your dog to get into trouble. Giving him too much freedom in your home before he is housetrained invites him to get into trouble and make mistakes. He will quickly develop the habit of eliminating in the wrong locations. It is far kinder to your dog to use management tools to keep him safe and prevent predictable accidents so he can enjoy more freedom later.

tethering maximizes your dog's opportunities for positive social interactions while also minimizing inappropriate behaviors.

During sessions of on-leash supervision, you can hold the leash in your hand or step on the end of it. You can also tether it to a stable piece of furniture or a well-secured eye hook as long as he cannot reach anything he might possibly damage. If you cannot keep your dog entertained, provide him with two chew toys (see the section on food-stuffed chew toys in Chapter Four on page 63) to keep him happily occupied. This arrangement is ideal when you are reading, relaxing in front of the TV, or working on the computer.

After approximately thirty minutes by your side (which can gradually be increased as your dog develops better bladder and bowel muscle control), it is likely that he will need to eliminate. Take him to his doggy toilet and reward him for being an extra smart pup and going in the right place.

After your dog has eliminated in the right spot and you are very confident that he won't make mistakes in the house, you can drop the leash and give him a bit more freedom as he plays with you. If necessary, you can quickly grab the leash if you see him heading out of your line of sight.

TRAINER'S TIP

What If My Pup Chews the Leash?

If you are diligent about providing your dog with at least two chew toys (see "Terms and Tools to Have in Your Trainer's Toolbox" on page 55), he will probably have little interest in chewing his leash. However, a few dogs find their leashes more enticing than the toys you have provided. In that case, remove the leash from your dog's mouth and gently hold it behind him so he can't reach it. When he relaxes, resume your preferred leashing or tethering method. It may require many repetitions before your dog learns that his leash disappears if he chews it, and he gets no attention from you or access to anything interesting. It's natural for dogs to mouth objects they find interesting, so you must be persistent. You should also reassess the toys you are offering. You may need to experiment until you find something that he finds more

In addition to a time management strategy to prevent mistakes and predict the need for elimination, you must learn to recognize the typical signals that indicate your dog's need to potty. These include sniffing, circling, and attempting to head to areas where elimination previously occurred. Some dogs, especially puppies under three months, have limited bladder and bowel control. They usually realize they need to go just moments before it happens and are therefore less likely to exhibit these behaviors.

Short-Term Confinement: Crate Training

Every dog needs to build bladder and bowel muscle control in order to be able to "hold it" for any significant period of time. Temporarily confining your dog to a small resting area, such as a crate, strongly inhibits the tendency to urinate and defecate, and therefore helps your dog build muscle control. Most dogs avoid soiling the crate. His time in the crate must be gauged according to his age, experience, and level of training. Most importantly, he must have adequate opportunities to be rewarded for eliminating elsewhere. Crate confinement also helps you to accurately predict when your dog needs to eliminate. If he has been napping or playing with his chew toys in his crate for a short period of time, it will be likely that he will need to eliminate

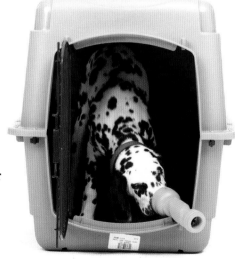

when he comes out. You can then take him to his designated doggie toilet and reward him for going in the right spot.

A crate is an invaluable housetraining and safety tool as long as it is combined with adequate potty breaks and sufficient mental and physical activity. It helps to prevent inappropriate chewing and teaches your dog to self-pacify when left alone. Crating is not only useful from a training standpoint; it's something every dog should be comfortable with. He will have to cope with it at the veterinarian, groomer, or when traveling, and these situations will become needlessly stressful if he is not trained to accept this.

To Crate or Not to Crate...That Is the Question

Ironically, teaching a pup to enjoy his crate can be easier than convincing pet parents to utilize this training tool. Responsible use of a crate should not be viewed as cruel and unusual punishment. It is comparable to using a playpen or crib to safely confine a child when he or she cannot be supervised.

When used properly, a crate facilitates housetraining and decreases destructive behavior. It accelerates your dog's overall training, which makes it possible to give him more freedom in safe areas of your home.

Your dog should perceive his crate as a positive retreat—never use it for punishment. It's a good place for your dog to spend a time-out as long as it is not paired with any verbal or physical reprimands. You can, however, use the crate to prevent potential misbehavior, such as housetraining mistakes, chewing, or dashing out the door when visitors arrive. However, long-term crate confinement is never a substitute for supervision and training. The objective is to help your dog develop good manners so that he can have freedom and enjoy time spent in your home.

After your dog is housetrained, you won't need to confine him to his crate. However, most dogs develop a strong attachment to their crates and enjoy this safe, private retreat. It is a good idea to keep your dog's crate in an accessible spot to ensure that he has a special place to rest and maintains his crate training skills. When it is used properly, your dog's crate becomes his special home within your home.

Placement of the Crate

It's not unusual for a new puppy or adult dog to feel initially distressed when making the transition to a different environment. In most cases, it is wise to allow the pup to sleep in your room near your bed, either in a crate or an exercise pen. This proximity helps the dog feel secure and calm. As he adjusts to his new home, you can gradually move his sleeping area farther away. You may prefer to have your dog sleep in bed with you once he is housetrained. Even so, every dog should learn to sleep alone without becoming stressed.

It's also a good idea to regularly move his crate to different locations in your home. This prevents him from associating it with isolation and introduces him to various household activities.

Regularly place your dog in his crate for short rest periods when you are home. This will prevent him from getting the idea that crate rest means that you will be leaving him for a prolonged period. This is equally important for small dogs that are being trained to use an indoor potty. Crate training also helps dogs build bladder and bowel muscle control, prevents inappropriate chewing, and encourages them to accept the idea of spending time quietly alone.

Crate Options

There are two types of crates: plastic and wire. Plastic crates are made of two interlocking pieces with ventilated sides and a wire door. Wire crates are made of folding panels with a removable bottom tray. Both styles have advantages.

Plastic crates are more den-like, and some dogs feel cozier and safer in them. They can also be used for air travel.

Metal crates can be folded for storage, and many come with a divider so the crate can be partitioned off to create a smaller sleeping area for a puppy. Metal crates can be covered with a blanket or towel to create more privacy for the dog. But some dogs will pull the fabric into their crate, so this should only be done when the dog is supervised.

Sizing

Choose an appropriate crate for your dog's size. He should be able to stand up, turn around, lie down, shift positions, and stretch. If the crate is too large, it may not inhibit elimination. He may urinate or defecate in one end and rest in the other. If you have purchased a crate in anticipation of your puppy's adult size, you can add a divider to make it temporarily smaller.

Introduction to the Crate

Dogs are descended from animals that instinctively seek dens to rest, stay safe, and wean their pups. But this doesn't guarantee that every dog will immediately accept the idea of being confined to a den-like area such as a crate. Follow these steps to help your dog become gradually accustomed to this invaluable training tool.

- Place the crate on the floor with the door open.
- Tie the door of the crate open so it won't accidentally shut and possibly frighten your dog.
- Do not place a pad, towel, or dog bed in the crate until you are confident that your dog will not chew it or urinate on this absorbent surface.
- Keep your dog on leash and have some tiny treats on hand.

Many dogs will investigate the crate without any prompting. If not, encourage him by placing a few treats inside. This is the first step to turning the crate into a "magic box." If you were given five hundred dollars every time you walked into a room, chances are you would soon love going there. The same holds true for your dog, except his version of five hundred dollars is food and toys.

After your dog has eaten the treats and steps out of the crate, ignore him for a moment. Next, place a few more treats in the crate, further toward the back. Gradually decrease the number of treats you toss into the crate, then wait for your dog to step toward or into the crate before tossing in another. Some dogs need a few practice sessions before they will enthusiastically enter the crate; others figure this out almost immediately.

When your dog is comfortably entering the crate on his own, change the procedure slightly:

- Toss treats to the back of the crate. Then, place yourself in front of the door and count to five before tossing in another treat. Repeat and gradually increase the count to fifteen. This teaches your dog to wait calmly in the crate for the arrival of the food reward.

- This first session with the door closed should take place after a period of play, exercise, and elimination. If your dog seems relaxed, close the crate door, toss in a treat, and count to five.
- When he is comfortable in the crate with the door shut for ten to fifteen seconds, begin to increase the duration of confinement. Provide him

  with a food-stuffed chew toy or toss in a piece of food every twenty to thirty seconds.
- When you open the door to let your dog come out, attach his leash and ignore him for a few moments while he stands quietly next to you. Repeat these steps many times, gradually increasing the amount of time that the door is closed. This teaches your dog that it can be rewarding to stay in the crate with the door closed.

- Once he seems relaxed in the crate with a chew toy and an occasional bit of food being tossed, begin moving a foot or two away from the crate as you watch TV, read a book, or work on your computer.
- When your dog has mastered this phase of crate training, start feeding him at least one meal a day in the crate, and begin using it as a resting place to encourage bladder and bowel muscle control. After he has spent time playing with his chew toys or napping in the crate, take him to his designated toilet area and reward him when he goes in the right spot.

Long-Term Confinement

During the initial stages of housetraining you should have an arrangement to confine your dog to ensure that he eliminates in a controlled area, like a

TRAINING TRUTH

How Much Time Should Your Dog Spend in His Crate?

A dog's natural instinct to avoid soiling his crate can be destroyed if he is left in the crate for long periods before he has developed sufficient bladder and bowel muscle control. He will be forced to soil the crate. Once he decides that it is okay to eliminate in his crate, housetraining him will become much more difficult. Place your dog in his crate after a successful potty break, when you are sure he is empty. As he develops better muscle control, you can gradually increase his time in the crate.

Crate Duration Guideline

Nine to ten weeks:	Approximately thirty to sixty minutes
Eleven to fourteen weeks:	Approximately one to two hours
Fifteen to sixteen weeks:	Approximately three to four hours
Seventeen or more weeks:	Approximately four or more hours (five hours maximum)

Your dog's ability to "hold it" while he is in the crate may vary. Most dogs are more willing to "hold it" for longer periods overnight. But when you begin the housetraining process—especially if you have a young pup—your dog may need to eliminate during the night. If so, set your alarm to wake you when you think your pup will need to go. Stay as calm and quiet as possible so your dog doesn't think it is playtime, take him to his potty area, calmly reward him for going, and then place him back in his crate.

Dogs need more potty breaks during the day when they are awake and more active. Your dog's ability to control his bladder and bowels will also be influenced by his activity level on a particular day (more activity usually means the need for more potty breaks). So, be prepared to vary your expectations accordingly.

nonporous floor covered with potty pads. This is essential when you must leave a puppy that is not housetrained for longer than he can reasonably hold it in his crate. It's also important if you have a small dog that will be using an indoor potty system permanently. In most cases, this is a temporary measure until your dog is old enough to hold it for longer periods of time in his crate, and eventually, for when he is free to roam around in your home. Your goal is to use this tool as briefly as possible to prevent your dog from developing a strong habit of eliminating indoors (even if on a designated surface).

Setting Up the Long-Term Area

An exercise pen is usually the ideal choice, but a bathroom or small kitchen will do. The long-term area should consist of a sufficient area for an indoor potty, a crate with the door left open as a sleeping area, and safe chew toys.

- Cover the entire floor of the long-term area with the chosen toileting surface (such as pads); this way your dog can't make any mistakes off the covered area and will develop a preference for going on a particular surface.

- After a week, leave a small section (approximately ten to twenty percent) of the floor uncovered. Begin removing the potty surface from areas nearest to his crate and where you are most likely to greet him. This encourages him to eliminate away from areas where he sleeps and minimizes the possibility that he will step in waste. If your pup has one accident off the intended substrate, re-cover the entire area and wait a few days before removing one or two pads. If ninety percent of the floor was covered and he chose to go on the ten percent that wasn't, he needs a little more time to develop a strong preference for this surface.

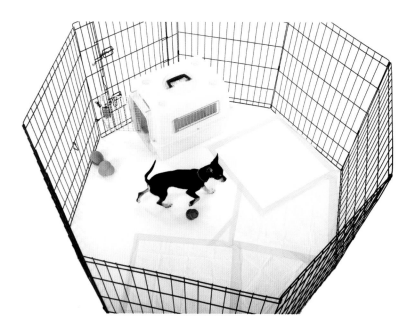

- If he doesn't make any mistakes for a few days, uncover a bit more. Continue until you are down to a square surface of substrate appropriate to your dog's size. If you want your dog to learn to go in a low-sided litter box, simply transfer the pads or paper there.

Unless you intend for your pup to be paper, pad, or litter box trained for life, he should have access to the indoor surface only until he is old enough to hold it for three to four hours in his crate. This is usually around four to five months old, but it depends on the individual dog and your diligence in helping him build muscle control with supervision and short-term crate confinement.

When he has developed sufficient control and can "hold it," confine him to his crate when you can't supervise him. Make sure that he has adequate relief walks throughout the day. Failure to do so is unfair and may cause a serious setback in housetraining.

The Good and the Pad

Indoor potties can be a temporary solution until a pup matures and has better bladder and bowel muscle control. They can also be

PAWS TO CONSIDER

Housetraining a puppy with an adult dog in the house requires separate rules and management routines for each dog. Rules for a sixteen-year-old would be different than those for an eight-year-old, and the rules and management tools vary for each dog. Don't feel guilty for this, especially since the ultimate goal is for your dogs to enjoy equal freedom in your home.

a lifelong choice for smaller dogs. In either case, there are some things to consider:

1. Puppies tend to adore shredding pads into confetti. To prevent this, use pads with adhesive strips or a pad holder.
2. Some dogs prefer to use certain substrates or filler surfaces for potty systems.
3. An indoor potty system should never become an excuse to avoid taking your dog out for exercise and socialization.

What Goes In on Schedule Comes Out on Schedule

Establishing a daily schedule helps your dog regulate his bathroom urges and makes it possible to predict when he will need to eliminate. During the housetraining process, it's important to keep track of details so you can remember when your dog needs to eliminate. Once he is house trained, you won't need to pay such close attention. Your dog will have the ability to "hold it" if his schedule gets a little off-track.

Food and Water

Free feeding is not recommended. It makes it more difficult to predict your dog's output, but this isn't the only reason to control your dog's access to food. It can be used to keep your dog occupied, or as a source of motivation during some training sessions. It also helps you to gauge your dog's appetite, which can be a tip-off when he isn't feeling well.

Feed him two or three times a day, and offer him water five to seven times. If your dog has unlimited access to both, he will probably need to eliminate constantly. His last feeding and watering should be at least two hours prior to his bedtime to minimize the possibility that he will need to eliminate during the night. Most dogs need a minimum of five elimination walks a day, but younger pups will need additional walks until they have developed the control to "hold it" for longer times between walks. Also, remember that after a period of play you need to take your dog to his designated potty spot because activity begets activity.

In the twenty-first century, most people lead very active lives outside the home. This is at odds with the requirements of a housetraining schedule, especially for a puppy that needs to eliminate frequently. A pup can't be expected to go all day without eliminating. So, a friend, neighbor, or pet care professional may need to be enlisted to help.

TRAINER'S TIP

Jackpot!

Elimination is a self-reinforcing behavior, meaning the act itself is rewarding for your dog as it offers relief. However, it is advisable to help your dog learn that eliminating in a designated area will also result in a virtual jackpot of rewards, including praise, treats, and play. Praise him calmly while he is eliminating, and more profusely afterward. Overly exuberant praise can distract your pup from the task at hand.

Transitioning from Indoors to Outdoors

When making the transition from indoor to outdoor potty training, the goal is usually to have the dog learn to eliminate exclusively outdoors. However, sometimes it is also possible to teach smaller dogs to eliminate outside in addition to an indoor potty. Both cases require restricting your dog's access to the indoor potty spot. This ensures that you will have plenty of opportunities to reward him for going outdoors. It means less time spent in the long-term confinement area, and more time spent resting in the short-term area or being supervised on leash.

Before you attempt to get your dog to eliminate outside on leash, spend a couple of days taking him to the indoor potty spot on leash. This gives him a chance to become comfortable eliminating on leash in front of you, which may be new for dogs that have been trained on an indoor potty spot. During this transition period, it is also advisable to carry your dog out so that accidents don't happen en route.

To help your dog develop a prompt elimination pattern when taken outside, take him to the same area of about 10 to 15 feet (3 to 4.6 meters) in width each time. Walk back and forth (as movement tends to get things going) for no more than five minutes, and stay as quiet as possible so he can focus on the task at hand, rather than on you.

Offer calm praise, a food reward, and a reward walk or play session after a successful potty break. If he doesn't eliminate within five minutes, carry him indoors, hold him for fifteen minutes (on your lap), and take him back out to try again. Be sure to not let him roam around when he comes in, as he may eliminate indoors. If this happens a few times, your dog will learn to go outside, sniff around, and then come back in to eliminate.

"Go Potty" Cue

Consistently taking your dog to his potty spot when he needs to eliminate should prompt him to go. However, you can add a verbal prompt, but don't do this until you are confident that your dog will eliminate within a few moments of reaching his spot. Use a word or phrase (such as "Go potty") just before he begins to go. This way, the word or phrase becomes connected with the act of eliminating through repetition. Refrain from saying this word or phrase until you can accurately predict when your dog will eliminate. If you say it and he doesn't eliminate, your dog will not learn to associate the word with the act.

Be calm and patient as your dog adjusts to eliminating on a new surface, in a new and potentially distracting environment. It generally takes no more than two or three trips outside in one session for a dog to eliminate, but some dogs require more time to adjust to this change in routine. This is usually due to a prolonged period of eliminating on an indoor surface or being punished for mistakes. A lack of adequate socialization and habituation may also result in a dog that is fearful and reluctant to eliminate when outdoors. In any case, plan outdoor potty breaks for those times when your dog will most likely need to eliminate (first thing in the morning) and in an area that is as quiet as possible.

Won't Wee on Walks

If a dog is sensitive to the environment and doesn't feel safe, he may not be able to relax enough to relieve himself. This is one reason why socialization is crucial to your dog's overall well-being and life skills. Try to identify things that worry him, and try to make him feel more comfortable. Plan his walks for times when he most needs to eliminate. Some dogs are reluctant to walk in the rain, so use an umbrella to protect him from the elements.

As your dog learns what he is meant to do when he heads outdoors, each trip will be quicker. Ultimately, he will eliminate promptly when taken outside rather than feel the need to walk around the block numerous times looking for the perfect spot. This is something you will definitely appreciate when you must walk your dog in inclement weather.

When your dog is reliably and promptly eliminating in one spot, begin to vary the location so that he learns to eliminate in other areas around novel stimuli.

Phasing Out Management Tools

One of the greatest challenges of house training is determining when your dog is ready to enjoy increased freedom in the home. The most common mistake pet parents make is prematurely assuming their dog is reliably housetrained. He will rapidly regress if you slack off the training routine when he is just starting to understand what is expected. A month or two of consistently eliminating in the appropriate spot rarely guarantees that a dog is housetrained. It usually means that he is in the process of developing a habit of elimination along with bladder and bowel control. For this reason, it is preferable to gradually increase his privileges rather than give him total freedom all at once.

Step One If your pup is consistently eliminating outdoors, phase out the use of paper, pad, or litter training and the long-term confinement area. This will be replaced by the use of the crate and on-leash supervision. You may also have to arrange for a responsible caregiver to take him out for elimination walks during this transition period.

Step Two When you are confident your dog has developed sufficient muscle control and will not eliminate in his crate for up to three hours, you can allow very brief periods (no more than fifteen minutes) of supervised play in a room that is safely dog-proofed. Be sure to provide him with two or three of his favorite chew toys to keep him busy.

Step Three Gradually increase these supervised periods when your dog is allowed to play with you and his chew toys in between walks.

Step Four Allow your dog brief periods of unsupervised time in a dog-proofed area while you are in the next room. Provide at least two engaging chew toys to keep him occupied. If your dog is not having housetraining or inappropriate chewing accidents, begin increasing the duration of these play times. Be sure to provide more outdoor potty breaks to ensure that he has adequate opportunities to eliminate in the right spot.

Learn for a Lifetime

Housetraining skills can deteriorate at any time in a dog's life, and management tools may need to be revisited. This is especially common when a dog is adjusting to more freedom in your home. Maintain his skills by continuing to offer occasional praise and a treat when he chooses the right spot. This is a great way to remind your dog that going in his designated doggy toilet is much more rewarding than going on the carpet.

DANGER!

Your dog may be so conditioned to going indoors that he will seek out surfaces like bath mats or piles of old newspapers when you remove the indoor potty area. You must be diligent about management during this transition period to ensure your dog's success.

Accidents Happen

By definition, a housetrained dog has a strong and reliable habit of eliminating in a specific area. However, occasional accidents may happen if a dog is under the weather, or if an owner fails to provide adequate walks. If accidents are not due to a medical condition, you will need to help your dog develop stronger housetraining skills by using some or all of the time management tools outlined in this chapter.

Never scold or punish your dog when he has an accident. This will most likely cause him to become fearful about eliminating in your presence. Simply clean up the mess, and use the incident as a reminder that you should better manage your dog's time to minimize future accidents.

Imagine if someone offered you one million dollars if you could prevent your dog from having housetraining mistakes for one month. Odds are that you would be diligent enough to make this happen. One million dollars is a strong incentive for housetraining success, but so is a housetrained dog.

Accident or Symptom?

Most housetraining issues are caused by inadequate management, failure to implement a realistic potty break schedule, or assuming that a dog is more reliable than he actually is. In some cases, the problem may be due to an underlying health issue, such as a urinary tract infection, diabetes, cystitis, functional incontinence, obesity, or internal parasites. If your dog is having housetraining accidents, especially if there is a sudden onset of mistakes, be sure to check with your veterinarian to rule out an underlying medical issue.

Effective Cleanup to Prevent Future Mistakes

If you are diligent about time management, accidents are far less likely to occur, but no dog is one hundred percent perfect. Mistakes will happen, and they must be thoroughly cleaned up to effectively remove odors that may entice your dog back to the area.

Do not reprimand your dog. Remove him from the area and place him in his long- or short-term area. Cleanup on a less porous surface, such as linoleum, is simple. Carpeted areas will require a bit more care. Avoid using household cleaners that only remove topical stains, especially those containing ammonia. To a dog, this smells somewhat like urine, and it may encourage him to repeat the act. Use a nontoxic pet stain remover that contains enzymes and safe bacteria to break down the scent. You can make your own pet cleaning solution from equal parts water or club soda mixed with baking powder, or distilled white vinegar mixed with equal parts water. In either case, be sure to test the solution on a small area of fabric to make sure it does not cause damage.

First, soak up the urine or remove the feces with paper towels, rinse with water, and then blot. Place the stain- and odor-removing solution on the soiled area and let it sit for the recommended period of time. In the case of a homemade solution, let it sit for a few minutes, dab up the excess, allow the area to dry and then vacuum.

Punishing Produces Plenty of Problems

A few things happen as a result of punishing your dog for accidents, none of which lead to housetraining success. Every time your dog has an opportunity to eliminate in the home, the habit becomes stronger. When you reprimand him for this, it is likely to send the message that you don't like to see him eliminate.

Dogs don't have the ability to understand what you are thinking, nor do they have the ability to understand being yelled at for one particular act (in this case, eliminating on the carpet in the living room). They don't think in terms of houses, expensive rugs, extra cleanup chores, or any other broad human concerns. Your dog is far more likely to process this scenario in very

TRAINER'S TIP

When a dog urinates upon greeting, it is called submissive or excitement urination. This indicates that the dog is sensitive and/or overexcited and needs to build self-confidence and self-control. Rather than adding to his state of excitement, ignore him for a moment or two when you enter a room. When you do approach, don't speak to him. Turn slightly away and avoid making eye contact. Try kneeling down instead of reaching over him and toss some treats on the floor.

simple terms: I got yelled at when I eliminated in front of this person, so they must not like it when I do that in front of them.

He may become reluctant to eliminate in your presence, but he will still need to go somewhere. He may be more likely to sneak off to relieve himself in forbidden areas and refuse to go when you take him for walks. This vastly complicates housetraining. Most importantly, constantly berating your dog will lead him to think that you aren't such a nice person after all.

The Myth of Spite and Guilt

Many owners believe that their dog eliminates in the home in retaliation for some perceived slight, such as being left home alone. They also believe that the dog feels supremely guilty for committing this act.

Neither spite nor guilt are parts of the canine emotional repertoire. In reality, indoor potty mistakes are due to a lack of adequate management, stress, or medical issues. The dog's "guilty" demeanor (ears and tail held low, cringing posture, and attempts to hide) when a puddle or pile is discovered is actually an expression of his fear of punishment, and an attempt to appease the potential punisher and minimize the stressful situation.

The end result is that the relationship between you and your dog is damaged, and your dog learns to hide from you (e.g., he eliminates behind the couch or when you are gone) when he needs to go. This is a common result of punishment training. What you are punishing for is not always what the dog thinks he is being punished for.

PAWS TO CONSIDER

Spay or Neuter

Spaying or neutering your dog may help to reduce territorial urine marking (when the dog produces small amounts of urine, most often directed at vertical surfaces and most common with intact adult males). Spaying will prevent females from bleeding during heat cycles and will also prevent or decrease uterine infections, breast and testicular cancer, some aggression issues, and roaming. Most importantly, it will prevent your pet from producing unwanted litters and adding to the pet overpopulation problem.

Socialization

L ife for a companion dog can be psychologically challenging because of the many things he must learn to cope with when living with humans. Companion dogs are often required to behave in ways that are counter-intuitive—even restrictive—which adds to their emotional challenges. Your dog will be better equipped to take things in stride if he has opportunities to become familiar with aspects of everyday life while he is young. A dog that is comfortable in his environment and accustomed to a variety of stimuli can be relied on to behave appropriately. As a result, his behavior becomes more predictable, which means he has fewer behavior issues. The door to the world can be opened wide for him to explore and participate in with confidence.

What Are Socialization and Habituation?

Socialization is the process of providing your dog with positive social interactions that will prepare him for experiences he will encounter throughout his lifetime. Primary socialization takes place with a pup's mother and littermates, and then with the pup's new human family. Secondary socialization involves people and animals outside the home.

Habituation is the process of providing continued exposure to stimuli over time. This helps your pup develop familiarity with his environment and teaches him to moderate his reactions to unfamiliar things. When a puppy is first exposed to things like traffic, vacuum cleaners, or loud voices, he is likely to wonder, *"What is that?"* Repeated, positive exposure helps him become comfortable around these things and learn to be confident when confronting other similar novelties.

Positive experiences via socialization and habituation help your dog to build a library of information that he can draw from when facing life's challenges. The larger the library, the better equipped he will be. A history of positive experience becomes his "social bumper," making him less sensitive and better able to bounce back from startling or unpleasant experiences.

A dog with limited positive exposure early in life is more likely to approach the world cautiously. A cautious canine will most likely be

stressed, fearful, and possibly aggressive when confronted by difficult situations. This resulting anxiety also inhibits his ability to learn. This in turn makes it increasingly difficult to teach the dog to become more relaxed and accepting.

Puppy Versus Remedial Adult Dog Socialization and Habituation

Although dogs have the capacity to learn throughout the lifetime, the process of socialization and habituation should ideally begin

PAWS TO CONSIDER

A dog's personality is the result of genetics (nature) and environment and experiences (nurture). By nature, some dogs are more inquisitive and jump right in to investigate new things. Others are genetically predisposed to be more cautious and reserved. They will sit back and watch while things "sink in." Each dog is an individual, and as such, will have particular preferences and responses. Regardless of this, socialization and habituation will help every puppy develop a degree of familiarity, tolerance, and enjoyment from a wide variety of people, places, things, and situations.

A dog with a fundamentally sound temperament still needs ongoing socialization to learn life skills. A dog that is genetically shy or timid needs loads of well-orchestrated socialization and habituation in order to successfully navigate life. The fearful pup of today is likely to become the aggressive dog of tomorrow.

during early puppyhood. The quality and quantity of a young puppy's experiences will influence his attitude and future behavior much more than subsequent experiences when he is older. Puppies that are deprived of early socialization and habituation often require considerable remedial work throughout their lifetime to become comfortable or tolerant of things they have not seen or done at a young age. Continued reinforcement of early, positive, formative social experiences should continue throughout your dog's adolescence, adulthood, and senior years. Great social experiences are as vital to your dog's well-being as a nutritionally complete diet.

Quantity or Quality?

The volume and variety of social experiences are important, but socialization is not just a numbers game. The quality of interactions and exposure are equally important factors. You should do your best to control what your puppy learns from each experience. Be selective and discerning so that he is gradually exposed to people, places, and things in a manner that encourages a positive, healthy response. The consequences of a bad experience can be far-reaching for some dogs, especially those with unstable temperaments. Keeping things positive is the key.

Socialization Begins at Home

After a puppy leaves his litter-mates and mother, his primary bond is with his human family. A puppy's secondary bonds are formed with people outside the home. At-home socialization should be part of your puppy's daily routine. However, you must be observant of signs that you are exposing the pup to more than he can cope with. This may be the case if he reacts with avoidance and extreme caution.

Handling and Gentling

One of the great joys of living with a dog is showing your affection for him through physical contact. There are similarities in the ways humans and canines express affection, such as proximity and play, but there are also major differences. For example,

TRAINING TRUTH

Safeguarding Your Pup's Mental and Physical Health

Puppy parents are sometimes confused by conflicting advice about keeping their young pup isolated or taking him out in a controlled setting before he has completed his vaccine schedule.

Young puppies are temporarily protected from diseases by the antibodies passed on to them through their healthy mother's milk. This gradually fades, and the pup begins producing his own antibodies. Outside the domestic setting, a pup would be exposed to diseases. If he survives, he develops protective antibodies against canine diseases. Vaccines stimulate the immunity that a dog would gradually develop through repeated exposure to diseases. Since the exact date when the maternal immunity fades is variable, puppies are given a series of vaccinations to ensure that they are protected.

In general, older pups have a more mature immune system that is capable of fighting off disease. However, the American Veterinary Society of Animal Behavior suggests that postponing socialization until a traditional vaccine schedule is complete can do more harm than good.

It is crucial to balance the need to protect your pup's physical health with his psychological well-being. This includes making sensible choices about his early socialization protocol. For example, a well-run, indoor puppy class where attendees are vaccinated poses a minimal risk to your pup's health. In fact, a class may pose less of a risk than a visit to the veterinarian's office, where the pup could be exposed to unhealthy dogs.

Your puppy's risk of contracting a disease is no more worrisome than his risk of developing into a distrustful, fearful, or aggressive adult because he was inadequately socialized. In general, puppies are more likely to recover from contagious diseases they might catch from other dogs than the long-term effects of inadequate early socialization. More dogs are euthanized due to behavior problems than die of distemper.

Avoiding contact with people outside of the home and other dogs may safeguard a puppy from exposure to contagious diseases, but it leaves him susceptible to ongoing behavior issues stemming from a lack of early socialization. Early, positive exposure to the world helps dogs adapt to everything they will be expected to accept throughout their lifetime.

many people enjoy hugging dogs, but many dogs aren't thrilled with this gesture. In dog language, the act of leaning over the shoulders, head, and back is a way of putting another dog in a more vulnerable or submissive position.

Similarly, when greeting people, we tend to walk straight toward them, look them in the eye, and reach out to shake their hand. Polite dogs tend to approach each other sideways, avert their gaze, circle, and sniff the other dog.

It's essential to accustom your dog to the typical ways that people express affection and perform grooming and health exams. This is especially important if the dog is going to live with children. Dogs deprived of this part of their education may become uncomfortable, stressed, and potentially aggressive in these common situations.

Most young pups will accept any type of handling, but this doesn't guarantee that they will be equally tolerant when they reach adulthood. You must proactively address this aspect of your puppy's training before problematic issues develop. Some dogs are less expressive in their affection and less tolerant of exuberant affection from people. Rather than being disappointed or offended, remember you have chosen to share your life with a different species. Be respectful of your dog's social boundaries and help him to gradually become more accustomed to our ways. This is accomplished through gentling and handling exercises.

Let the Handling Games Begin!

Schedule brief daily handling and gentling sessions for a time when your puppy is usually comfortable. Offer him things he likes most (such as food) to help him develop a positive attitude about being handled.

Start by gently touching one part of your puppy's body while you offer a tiny treat, or let him lick from a food-stuffed toy. Plenty of daily repetitions will result in your puppy happily accepting a touch because he will learn

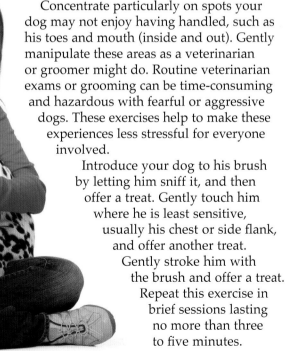

to associate it with the prospect of a yummy food treat.

Concentrate particularly on spots your dog may not enjoy having handled, such as his toes and mouth (inside and out). Gently manipulate these areas as a veterinarian or groomer might do. Routine veterinarian exams or grooming can be time-consuming and hazardous with fearful or aggressive dogs. These exercises help to make these experiences less stressful for everyone involved.

Introduce your dog to his brush by letting him sniff it, and then offer a treat. Gently touch him where he is least sensitive, usually his chest or side flank, and offer another treat. Gently stroke him with the brush and offer a treat. Repeat this exercise in brief sessions lasting no more than three to five minutes.

Rollover

Teaching your pup to roll over for examination should not be confused with an alpha roll, which is physically forcing the puppy to lie on his back as a submissive gesture. Rather than teaching the puppy to be submissive, that approach is likely to encourage a confrontational attitude. However, teaching your pup to willingly roll over is an excellent way to ensure that examinations will be easy. This exercise also helps your pup to develop trust in you and confidence in himself, because he learns to feel safe and comfortable in a potentially vulnerable position.

Begin by sitting on the floor and holding your pup in your lap. Gently tickle or scratch his belly and chest to encourage him to open his flank and expose his belly. Offer a tiny food treat, or allow your pup to lick from a food-stuffed toy.

- Repeat in three- to five-minute sessions until your pup is completely relaxed.
- Gently place your pup on the floor and repeat the same process.
- Have different family members practice this exercise with the pup in different areas of your home. Children can assist in exercises like this if they can follow instructions and are suitably gentle, but they should always be supervised.

- Invite friends to practice the exercise with your pup, one at a time. Always supervise and instruct them on how to handle your pup gently to ensure that they reinforce the foundation you have set.

"Gotcha" Game

Being able to quickly grab your dog makes daily life much easier, and it's essential in an emergency. Many dogs dislike being grabbed by the collar because they associate this with punishment. Teach your dog to not only tolerate, but also happily accept, collar grabs by playing the "gotcha" game. Do this at least twenty-five times a day. Each repetition takes no more than three seconds. Reach down and place one finger in his collar as you say *"Gotcha!"* and offer him a tasty treat. Gradually grab his collar more firmly in order to build up his tolerance to the type of grab you might do in an emergency. Frequently interrupt play and other activities to do a collar grab.

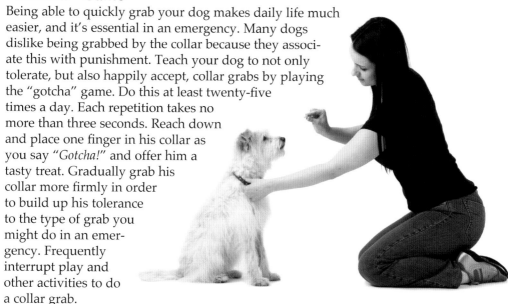

Restraint

Teaching your pup to tolerate and even enjoy being restrained ensures that you will be able to do this safely and easily without his struggling to get free.

- Sit on the floor and hold your pup on your lap.
- Gently put your hands around or under your dog's chest, hold him loosely for two to three seconds, and offer a treat.
- Gradually increase the length of the loose hold, and calmly massage your pup's chest.
- Decrease the length of the hold as you gradually increase the intensity. Continue to reinforce with food for each hold.
- When your pup accepts this exercise calmly, gradually increase the duration again.

If your pup struggles, it means that you have exceeded his tolerance threshold. Decrease the duration and/or intensity of the restraint, and offer more frequent rewards until he learns to willingly accept this handling. Practice in many different places and enlist the assistance of family and friends to help your pup become a hug-happy hound.

Object Exchange

Both dogs and people can get into the habit of guarding valuable resources. We might be excused for reprimanding someone who touches our valuables, but this response is not tolerated by our dogs. They must learn to show impeccable self-control when humans take things away from them.

Don't wait until your dog takes something you don't want him to have before you address this issue. Help your dog feel good about the idea of having things taken away. Start by trading rather than taking.

Give your dog a low-value toy, take it away, give him a treat, and then give the toy back.

If your dog is looking at you pleasantly and expectantly at this point, move on to a toy of higher value in future sessions and be ready to offer some jackpot rewards. In this way, your dog learns that giving up a valued object means he will get it back with interest!

Food Bowl Fun

Whether your dog eats from a food-stuffed toy or a bowl, he should become comfortable with people taking this object away.

- Start with your dog on leash tethered to a stable object.
- Place an empty bowl or toy on the floor in front of him and immediately reach to take it away. Then offer your dog a piece of food.
- Repeat several times. When he is comfortable with this exercise, begin tossing bits of food into the bowl prior to taking it away.
- Practice walking by him and tossing food into the bowl; this way, he will learn to appreciate your approach when he is eating. Gradually approach from a greater distance and get closer to your dog.

Dogs and Children

This area of socialization deserves special attention. A dog can have a profound impact on the life of a child. This can include learning to be kind, gentle, and empathetic. Friendship with a dog can help a child build confidence and learn responsibility. Dogs can also facilitate social interactions with others. After all, few things make it easier to strike up a conversation than having your dog by your side.

However, dogs may have a difficult time adjusting to children because they look, act, and sound different from adults.

Preparing for the Arrival of a New Baby

Help your dog prepare for the big event by following these steps:

- Plan a veterinary visit to make sure your dog is healthy. Arthritis or an infected paw or ear can make him more irritable.
- Work with a trainer to improve your dog's manners and responsiveness to requests.
- Prepare your dog for less attention by helping him improve his self-pacifying skills.
- Teach your dog to rest calmly in a confined area (crate, ex-pen, or separate room).
- Hold a doll swaddled in a towel and play a tape of a baby crying so your dog will be accustomed to these stimuli when the baby arrives.
- Condition your dog to accept the type of behavior typical from a child.
- Work on anti–resource guarding exercises to ensure that your dog does not begin to covet toys when the baby arrives.
- Be prepared for the possibility of stress that may lead to housetraining mistakes, increased attachment behaviors (such as following you around), and excessive barking.
- As the baby matures, management must be even more diligent. Your dog must be protected from your child and vice versa. Even the most patient dog can be pushed beyond his threshold for tolerance and pain.
- If your dog walks away from your child, discourage the child from following by redirecting him. If the dog is walking away, he wants social distance.
- Create a blocked-off area where your dog can eat, drink, and rest undisturbed.

Most children are experts at ramping up the level of energy in a room, and dogs often respond to this in ways that are normal for dogs but considered unacceptable by people. Furthermore, young children may not possess the requisite skills, awareness, and consideration necessary for safe, fun play with dogs.

Dogs and children speak different languages. The best way to establish a successful relationship between kids and dogs is by providing constant supervision, and teaching them how to behave around each other. Carefully supervised experiences with well-mannered children are an important part of every puppy's socialization.

If you don't have children, arrange for your puppy to have interactions with well-mannered children as often as possible. If you have children, they should have a role in your dog's daily routine, with consistent adult supervision. Depending on their age and personality, children can help with some or all of the following tasks:

- Refreshing the dog's water.
- Stuffing toys with food prior to mealtimes and giving the dog these toys.
- Practicing exercises such as *sit* and hand targeting, and the *pass and drop* game, where the child walks by the dog and drops a tiny piece of food for him to pick up.

Teaching children how to interact with dogs should include:

- Inviting the dog to come to you rather than approaching

DANGER!

No breed or individual dog can be expected to be consistently tolerant and gentle with children. Even the most friendly, stable dog can be overwhelmed by a child's running, squealing, and grabbing. For this reason, interactions between children and dogs should always be supervised by an adult.

him. This allows the dog to choose to interact, rather than be forced to do this.

• Talking to the dog in a controlled voice to avoid overexciting or startling him.
• Refraining from roughhousing, teasing, chasing, or encouraging the dog to chase them.
• Allowing the dog to eat and sleep undisturbed.
• Holding the dog only when seated and supervised.

It is often easiest for kids to remember catch phrases when learning the rules for a successful canine-kid relationship:

• **Four on the Floor**: The dog must have four paws on the floor when saying hello.
• **Chew Toy Charm**: Chew toys work like a charm when teaching your dog to be charming and polite.
• **Tether Time-Outs**: Tethering the dog during supervised interactions with the kids allows them to easily step away if needed.

Meeting People Outside the Home

Allowing your puppy to become overly attached to you can inhibit his sense of independence and his ability to self-pacify, resulting in separation issues. He should have a balance of personal attention, time spent alone resting and playing with chew toys, and social interactions outside your family group.

Consistent socialization helps him build confidence and develop positive associations about all things human.

To accomplish this, he should have regular exposure to:

- people of all ages, races, sizes, shapes, and gender;
- people with varying types of facial hair, and people wearing hats, uniforms, or heavy winter coats; and
- people carrying or using items such as umbrellas, walkers, or strollers.

Without positive, repeated exposure, even the friendliest dog may be startled or frightened by some of these things. Consider yourself a social director responsible for coordinating varied social interactions for your pup.

Take your pup for frequent visits to your vet's office at times other than when his veterinary exam is scheduled. This gives him opportunities to meet and greet people and learn that the vet's office is often a place to get tasty treats and make new friends. You should also follow this procedure if you plan to take your dog to a professional groomer.

Socializing is an art form that some people master better than others. The same holds true for dogs. Provide your dog with the best chance to have a large, admiring social circle by teaching him that meeting people calmly is a rewarding experience. However, it is sometimes difficult to control the interactions your pup may have with various people he meets in public. Most people who approach to interact with him will have little awareness of how their behavior affects him. They may frighten him by squealing with excitement or by approaching rapidly, or they may encourage him to mouth on their fingers! It's your responsibility to manage the quality of your pup's social interactions.

First and foremost, do not allow anyone to approach your puppy unless that person is willing or able to make eye contact with you and heed your instructions.

Second, explain that you are teaching your pup to enjoy greeting people; and let the person know you would appreciate his or her assistance. The person may simply want to pet or admire your dog rather than help you to reinforce his manners. But, the privilege of interacting with your dog should be contingent on the person's willingness to help.

Explain that he or she must stand or kneel, be still and calm, and allow your pup an opportunity to choose to approach. Let the person know you will step on the leash to inhibit jumping, but if his paws leave the ground, the person should turn, step, and look away from the dog. When he has four paws on the floor, the person can turn around, offer a treat you have provided, and calmly say hello.

If your pup doesn't step forward when he meets someone, he is saying loud and clear that he doesn't feel safe. Never lift the pup up and place

PAWS TO CONSIDER

During the socialization process, a pup may exhibit a sudden onset of fear or reserved behavior. Behavior is constantly changing, especially during critical developmental periods like transitions from puppyhood to adolescence and then adulthood. Socialization must be ongoing throughout a dog's adult life because it can wear off without continued exposure to a wide range of things.

him close to another person or dog. This is disrespectful and inconsiderate of his feelings. He should only be required to have close contact with people and animals he feels comfortable with. Forcing interactions in this way could lead to fear and aggression.

If your pup is hesitant to approach a stranger, give the person some treats to offer him. If that doesn't work, move on and make note that you need to work on this issue with friends in a controlled setting like a training class.

The Great Outdoors

It's a great big world out there and your dog can have a wonderful future experiencing all it has to offer. But this can't happen unless you help him become tolerant of the things that might otherwise cause concern. Some of the things your dog may need to become comfortable with include:
- Moving Vehicles: cars, trucks, motorcycles, skateboards, bikes
- Different terrain and weather conditions: grass, concrete, sand, metal, wood, snow, and rain

- Unfamiliar places: training class, pet supply stores, local parks, outdoor cafés and shopping malls, the veterinarian's office, a grooming shop, other people's homes, elevators, and stairs
- Unusual sounds: hair dryer, vacuum, brooms, washing machines, food processors, garbage disposal, lawn mowers, and even people arguing.

It's normal for a puppy to be startled by an unfamiliar sound. Prevent this reaction from escalating into a fear or phobia by providing him with repeated exposure to different sounds while offering rewards like food, toys, and play to help him make a positive association.

Other Dogs

Dogs must learn the art of proper social behavior with their own species. Puppies typically have plenty of interaction with their own species playing with their mother and littermates. After they go to a new home, they also need opportunities to continue practicing these canine social skills throughout puppyhood and adolescence. To do this, they need regular interactions with dogs of different ages and sizes.

Without these experiences a dog may become incapable or unmotivated to relate to his own species. As a result, he may become anxious, irritable, and possibly aggressive when meeting other dogs on the street or in a veterinarian's office. Dogs can develop special friendships. But, in most cases, it is advisable to avoid them. A dog that becomes overly dependent on a single canine friend may become reluctant to engage in a wider circle of social interactions.

Playing with older dogs helps a puppy learn good play manners. Adult playmates should be relatively tolerant of puppy exuberance and know how to discipline a rowdy pup without inflicting any damage. Young puppies are usually allowed a lot of leeway by well-socialized adult dogs. However, by the time pups have reached four to six months of age, their "puppy license" expires. If your pup has not learned good manners with other dogs at a young age when "rudeness" is generally more permissible, it's likely that an adult dog will eventually take exception to his behavior. At this point, most adult dogs become less forgiving of a younger dog's overly exuberant behavior and may correct him. This might include a hard stare, stiff body, turned head, growl, or an air snap.

Greeting dogs on leash in public places is generally not the best way for them to interact. An overly enthusiastic reaction may be considered rude by the other dog, leading to aggressive retaliation. The leash also inhibits body language that is meant to keep the interaction friendly. In fact, a tight leash may encourage aggression because the dog may feel threatened and unable to move a safe distance away. If the dog has no opportunity to get away from a threatening situation, he may react defensively and fight.

Allowing your dog to greet others on the street can also undermine his training. Rather than walking politely on the leash, he may get into the habit of pulling toward dogs. Off-leash play in safely enclosed areas is the best option.

Dog Parks

Dog parks can provide a wonderful physical and social outlet for dogs and their people. However, the inability to ensure that all dogs are well socialized or properly supervised makes these environments potentially risky, especially for puppies, adolescents, and more tentative adult dogs. If you want to take a pup or timid dog to a dog park, choose times when they are less crowded, such as early mornings on the weekend or midday during the week.

Play Styles

Every dog has his own way of engaging in play. Some like to chase, while others prefer to be chased. Some dogs tend to lie on the floor and mouth another dog, while others prefer standing up and wrestling with their paws. While style and intensity may vary, play sessions always include some actions that replicate fighting, predatory behavior, and reproductive displays, such as shoulder pawing, raised hackles, brief periods of mounting, and teeth displays. This can make it challenging to distinguish between play and real fighting. A baseline understanding of your dog's play style will help prevent impending trouble. This is a reason why trainer-moderated play groups can be beneficial. An expert pair of eyes can help you recognize the signs of normal, safe dog play.

If you are worried that a play session may be escalating into an actual fight, ask yourself the following questions:

1. Is either dog bothered by the interaction?
2. Are both dogs choosing to continue, or is one trying to escape?
3. If you are concerned that a pup may need to be "rescued" from a play encounter, remove the dog that seems to be bullying and hold him off to the side for a moment. It is a false alarm if the pup approaches his restrained companion to reengage in play.

Play should include a combination of excitement and self-control. Most healthy, safe dog play is interspersed with moments when one or both dogs attempt to tone things down. They send out reminder signals, such as a play bow, to say that this is all meant to be in good fun. They might also temporarily disengage from play and signal this by slowing down their movements, lying down, sitting, rolling over, or averting their gaze.

Similar to a sports game, even the most exuberant and physical athletes must play by the rules for the game to continue. In this case, each dog has his own rules, and these will vary depending on whether the playmate is a close canine buddy or a potential new friend.

A dog with superb social skills is able to temper or modify his play behavior according to a playmate's play style. In addition to bite inhibition, many well-socialized dogs will modify other aspects of their body language and posture. Large dogs may flop to the ground to play with a smaller dog or be less likely to wildly chase. In many cases, the appropriateness of play interaction between two dogs is governed by their play style and abilities to modify their behavior rather than the size or age of the dogs.

It is usually obvious if a dog's arousal level reaches a point at which he is losing the ability to modify and/or inhibit his behavior during play. When this happens, it is your responsibility to step in like a referee in a sports game, because a time-out from play is in order.

Puppy Training Classes and Play Groups

Puppies that receive early socialization and attend classes are more likely to remain with their families and to experience a happier overall life. A good puppy class can help to instill desirable behaviors, such as paying attention; following, *sit, down, stand*, handling, hand targeting, and recall; settling with a chew toy; and acquiring anti-resource guarding skills.

In addition to socialization with dogs and people, classes are an opportunity to practice training skills around distractions such as other dogs. Play

sessions with other dogs in the class can be used as a reward for responding to requests. For instance, when the puppy *sits* he may be rewarded with off-leash play.

The trainer should outline the expectations, rules of engagement, and potential consequences. He or she should also provide running commentary on what's going on during playtime and intervene often to prevent the puppy from becoming a victim or a bully. Much of this involves redirection until reciprocal play is happening.

A well-structured and organized puppy class can be one of the most beneficial experiences for a new pup and his family. However, puppy classes should not be the extent of your puppy's education or exposure to people and other dogs outside the home. It is the first step in your puppy's ongoing education and a supplement to socialization that should take place every day.

Your puppy's social interactions should be carefully monitored, but don't become overly protective. Every puppy needs opportunities to work through typical social interactions with dogs. As long as there is little risk of injury between pups of similar size and play styles, these experiences will help your pup develop self-confidence.

Other Animals

Contrary to popular belief, dogs, cats, and other animals can become amiable companions and even playmates. It is important that both animals, especially the one most likely to inflict potential damage (usually the dog), know how to play without frightening or endangering the other animal. The play should end when either one wants to stop.

Introductions to cats and other small animals should take place after the dog has had a chance to burn off a good bit of steam with some appropriate exercise.

The dog should be kept on leash and repetitively redirected to pay attention to you using hand targeting and other basic manners skills. This not only curbs any inclination to overexcitement; it also provides a way to constantly evaluate your dog's state of mind and ability to focus on something other than the encounter with another animal.

Remedial Socialization

Fear is an unpleasant state of mind for any dog, and it is at the root of a myriad of behavior issues. It can be due to genetics, inadequate socialization and habituation, an unpleasant experience, or a combination of these factors. Some dogs have a specific phobia, such as a fear of men with beards. Others have a more general fear of the world at large. In some cases, fear of one particular person, place, thing, or sound can become associated with something else. This is known as generalization or fear by association. This can happen if your dog perceives two stimuli as similar or links them because he was exposed to both at the same time. For example, if your dog is afraid of loud truck noises and hears this sound at the same time that he sees a child, he may develop a similar fear of children.

The reactive response of growling, barking, or lunging is often motivated by fear, and the dog is attempting to keep the scary thing at a distance. In these situations, some owners are inclined to avoid exposing their dog to people, places, or things that make the pup apprehensive. However, this

DANGER!

Never force your dog into encounters he is not equipped to handle when you are helping him to overcome a fear. If he becomes too frightened, his fight-or-flight instinct may take over. If he is prevented from avoiding the fearful situation, he may instead behave aggressively in an effort to increase social distance and protect himself. Exposure to stimuli that is too intense can backfire and make the dog more fearful rather than help him to adapt. Whether you have a young pup or a mature dog, the goal is to help him gradually gain confidence and a greater sense of comfort. During these exercises, always watch for signs of stress, such as avoidance, averting his eyes, whimpering, or shaking.

approach is likely to exacerbate the fear. A program to modify this fear will require time and effort, but it is well worth it in the long run.

The protocol to help your dog overcome a fear is accomplished through a methodical program of creating a new, positive association for him between the source of his fear and the things he values and enjoys. The first step is to identify things that give your dog confidence and enjoyment. These will be offered to him as he is gradually exposed to the thing he fears.

Dogs that display a tentative reaction to something fearful should be allowed to maintain the space they need to feel safe. Never force your dog to approach or interact with a person he is afraid of. His exposure to the source of his fear should never reach a point where he exhibits fear. Gauge your dog's fear threshold by offering him something he truly enjoys. If he doesn't take it, lower the intensity of his exposure until he is comfortable taking the toy or treat. This is the current threshold of his tolerance in this situation.

The first practice sessions should take place when your dog is hungry, so that food treats will have the most reinforcement value for him. At first, he should have very mild exposure to the source of his fear.

Plan for repeated exposure at this low intensity. Gradually increase the intensity of exposure as he learns to associate things he loves with the presence of the scary thing.

When the scary thing goes away (for example, when the person moves farther away), stop giving him reinforcements.

If he is fearful of visitors, start by introducing him to one friend who is ready, willing, and able to follow your detailed instructions for this remedial socialization program.

- The person should remain calm, maintain non-threatening body language, be sitting or kneeling and facing sideways to the dog, and take care to avert his or her eyes and face.
- During these sessions, avoid too much conversation between yourself and the person. The person's voice might add to your dog's fear response.

- Make sure that the encounter never exceeds your dog's threshold for comfort. That is, if the dog will take food from you when the visitor is 10 feet (3 meters) away, keep the visitor at least 11 feet (3.4 meters) away.
- Ask the visitor to drop high-value treats on the ground so the dog can approach to sniff and eat when he feels safe doing this. At first, this may require tossing the treat a good distance away before the dog will feel safe approaching to take it.
- Gradually decrease the distance of the toss so the dog must come closer to get the food. In most cases, the dog will approach and then retreat. With repeated exposure in this way, your dog will learn that this person is the most rewarding game in town.
- When the dog seems ready, ask the visitor to calmly extend his or her hand and offer the dog a treat from an open palm.
- Over the course of many sessions, repeat this exercise in other rooms of the home, then outdoors, and eventually with different helpers.
- When the dog is consistently approaching the person to accept food from an open hand, go to the next step. Begin helping your dog accept the idea of someone approaching. Start by asking the person to take a step or two toward the dog from the side, keeping his or her gaze averted. Then kneel to the dog's side and offer food from his or her hand or by tossing it on the ground.
- If the dog is fearful with a particular adult member of the family, practice this exercise and also have this person feed, walk, and offer special toys and treats to the dog. This formerly scary person will be transformed into someone the dog can trust and depend on for the things he wants and needs. During this process you may need to limit the dog's interactions with other family members if this bond is inhibiting the dog's ability to form trusting relationships with others.
- As the dog becomes confident about food, toys, and attention from someone other than his preferred person, he will build a trusting bond with a broader social circle of humans.

If your dog is afraid of other dogs, use a similar protocol to help him overcome this problem.

- Begin by exposing him to dogs that are calm and slightly smaller.
- Gradually introduce him to larger dogs and/or those with a more active demeanor.
- Teach your dog to respond to a few requests (such as *sit* and hand targeting). Once your dog has learned that these are rewarding endeavors, they can be used to help him focus on something rewarding during these exercises to overcome fear.

Remember, when working with fearful dogs, it's best to use requests rather than to issue forceful commands (assuming the dog understands what is being asked of him).

Dog Training 101: Foundation Exercises

In the dog training world, the term "obedience" traditionally refers to teaching dogs to perform a behavior on cue, such as *sit, lie down*, and *come when called*, as well as more advanced skills like retrieving on command. However, in real-life situations these behaviors are more accurately described as manners or life skills. Life skills help your dog respond appropriately in different situations. His reliable behavior keeps him safe and makes it possible for him to enjoy the mental, physical, and social stimulation that comes with more freedom. Mannerly behavior is the natural result of a trusting and cooperative relationship that comes from having your dog on a "Learn to Earn" program (see page 34).

Specific Versus Generalized Learning

Many dogs respond perfectly to requests at home, but they seem to develop selective hearing once you hit the streets or a local park. This is because environment has a big impact on behavior. Your behavior changes somewhat when you are in a work environment or a casual setting with friends. Random factors and distractions in an environment can influence your dog's behavior, but this isn't the only factor to consider. Dogs typically learn things within a specific context, and it is not easy for them to apply the concept to different situations. For example, your dog may learn to respond reliably to the cue to *sit* when practicing in your living room. He may not respond so readily in the park unless you have

TRAINER'S TIP

Spend a few moments each morning prepping yourself to be your dog's teacher. Prepare three to five food-stuffed toys, a treat pouch containing at least three varieties of finely diced food rewards, small jars filled with tiny treats placed in different rooms (out of your dog's reach), one or two squeaky toys, and a 6-foot (1.8-meter) leash. Handy access to these items ensures that you make the most of training opportunities throughout the day.

practiced in this setting.

Once your dog has mastered basic training skills at home, he should have opportunities to practice them in varying environments and contexts in order to help him generalize these concepts. Help your dog build his learning muscles through loads of repetitions. Rewards also help him learn to ignore potential distractions. This is how basic obedience exercises are translated into useful life skills that your dog can use in any situation.

Identify situations that are most challenging for your dog, and plan controlled practice sessions that will gradually accustom him to respond in that environment. If your dog does not respond to a request, he may be confused or anxious. Maybe you are expecting too much of him, and he needs practice to improve his reliability.

Layers of Learning

Learning to use skills like *sit, down,* and *stay* in a dog's daily life is a step-by-step process. It begins with teaching him to respond to a cue or request and then generalizing his understanding of the cued behavior. There are five stages or layers to achieving this goal.

Stage One Stage one consists of helping your dog learn the behavior in a controlled, limited context. In this phase, getting the desired behavior to happen is the goal. It doesn't matter if your dog doesn't respond perfectly to *sit*. If he displays the behavior for a moment, it warrants a reward to ensure that he will repeat the behavior in hopes of getting more rewards. In most cases, food is the most effective reward; it is highly valued by most dogs and can be used for rapid repetition during a practice session. The dog can consume tiny food rewards quickly and refocus on the next task. It is important to reward every correct response during this stage. For example, if your dog *sits* in response to a hand signal in the living room he should receive a tiny food reward each time.

Stage Two The next step is teaching your dog a verbal cue for the behavior. Say it just before the behavior happens or the visual cue is given. As before, he should receive a reward for each response.

Stage Three When your dog is responding reliably to the cue (in this case, "*Sit*"), begin to vary elements of the exercise. This includes practicing in different parts of your home, varying the duration of the exercise and the dog's distance from you, and introducing distractions. These things will help your dog to develop a generalized understanding of the cue in a controllable situation. Continue giving your dog food rewards for each response. However, some dogs may respond better if you use a variable rate of reinforcement.

Stage Four At this stage, the cued behavior is phased into real-life situations. Continue to provide food rewards, but vary this with other rewards, such as toys, the opportunity to walk through a doorway or gate, or an invitation onto the couch for each correct response. Your dog's access to rewards of all kinds now becomes contingent on responding to cues.

Stage Five By this stage your dog will have had hundreds of opportunities to practice the behavior in varying situations, with varied rewards. You should expect a reliable rate of response in multiple environments. However, rewards and practice are still required to maintain a good response rate. If you rest on your laurels, his new skills are likely to deteriorate or disappear.

How to Make Behaviors Happen

As discussed in Chapter 3, there are a number of ways to make a behavior happen. The methods of choice are:

Luring Luring can be a great way to get a behavior started. Hold a treat or toy in front of your dog's nose and move it to entice him to follow. You can maneuver him into a desired position using this method.

Capturing Capture a behavior your dog offers spontaneously by marking and rewarding him whenever it happens. This is a super fun and fast approach to help your dog become fully engaged in the training game.

Shaping Shaping rewards your dog for actions that approximate the behavior you are trying to teach. This method raises the standard in small steps in which your dog reliably learns to perform the behavior. It is best for teaching more complex behaviors, such as spinning, rolling over, or fetching.

Marker A marker sound (such as a clicker or the word "*Yes*") allows you to give specific, focused feedback to your dog. The sound tells him that whatever he did at the moment he heard the sound will earn a reward. A marker sort of bridges the time between the instant the behavior happens and the arrival of the reward. When your dog makes this connection, he is likely to repeat the behavior to make both the sound and the reward happen again.

Using a marker, especially a clicker, can greatly accelerate your dog's rate of learning. Prior to using the marker, you need to teach your dog that the sound means a reward is forthcoming. To do so:

- Make the marker sound and give a treat.
- Repeat until your dog looks at you with an expression of anticipation when he hears the marker sound. Most dogs have a "lightbulb" or "Aha!" moment after ten repetitions.
- Do not reach into your treat pouch or pocket prior to clicking, or you may distract your dog from the task. Ideally, your treats should eventually be out of view to avoid training your dog to comply with your requests only when treats are in view.

PAWS TO CONSIDER

Positive training is about putting your dog in a position to make the right decision, allowing him to make his decision, and using the marker to reward him for making the right choice. Doing so consistently results in a strong, reliable understanding of appropriate behavior. The more you reward a behavior, the more likely it is to occur in the future. These behaviors do not always have to follow a cue. If your dog sits politely to greet someone, regardless of whether you cued him to *sit*, reward him to ensure that he will repeat this response the next time someone approaches to say hello.

If your dog is sensitive to the sound of the clicker, you can muffle it by holding it under your shirtsleeve, or by using a ballpoint pen to make a similar sound. A verbal marker like the word "*Yes*" can also be used.

Release Word When using a marker, the sound tells your dog that he has completed the required task to earn the reward. In this way, it also releases him from that action. However, you should also use a release word or phrase, such as "*Okay*" or "*All done*," to indicate that the exercise is over and your dog can relax until further notice. This is useful when behaviors are established and you no longer need to use the marker.

Adding Cues Positive trainers tend to use the words "cue" or "request" instead of "command," which implies an attitude of "you better do it or else!" Positive trainers also ensure that cues only be added when they are confident that the behavior will happen. This way the dog develops a strong connection between the two. If your dog does not respond to the

cue, resist the urge to repeat the word multiple times. In most cases, a failure to respond correctly is because too much is being asked of the dog at his level of training.

Consistency of Cues Decide which verbal and visual cues you want to use, and make sure the whole family sticks with them. Changing cues, even subtly, can confuse your dog. For example, if you teach your dog to *sit* in response to "*Sit*," don't expect him to respond to "*Sit down*."

Tenor of Your Voice There is no need to modify your voice to make it sound more authoritative or demanding when giving your dog verbal cues or requests. Speak in your normal tone during training sessions so that your dog will learn to respond to friendly requests in real life.

Size, Quantity, and Type of Food Rewards Food rewards can be highly effective because they are something your dog wants, and you can vary them from low to high value depending on the challenge of the task at hand. Food rewards are especially useful during the early stages of training. Later, they can be used variably in conjunction with other rewards, such as toys, praise, and access to other things your dog wants. Plan your dog's first few training sessions just prior to his mealtime so that he is hungry and eager to play the game.

Treats should be about fingernail-sized so they are easy to consume, which makes it possible to repeat promptly. Avoid crumbly treats so that your dog doesn't spend more time vacuuming the floor than concentrating on the lesson at hand.

Before training sessions, chop up a variety of food rewards into tiny pieces so you are prepared to reinforce behaviors you like throughout the day. Chat with your veterinarian about foods that are appropriate for your dog. This may include commercial dog treats, boiled chicken or turkey, cheese, air-popped popcorn, carrots, and other vegetables. You can reduce your dog's normal meals by about twenty percent so that you can substitute with healthy treats throughout the day.

Reap Rewards from Repetition Just like physical muscles, learning muscles grow stronger through repetition. Numerous brief repetitions produce the longest-lasting results. When you begin teaching any new behavior, pick a place and time where distractions are minimal; this ensures that your dog's ability to focus on you and the lesson at hand is at a maximum. Gradually and consistently incorporate these lessons into daily life.

Length of Sessions It is generally best to schedule three- to five-minute sessions at first. Both you and your dog will find it easier to focus and

BETTER BEHAVIOR

If you are still working on teaching your dog to take food gently from your hand, don't overlook this expectation of good manners when you are rewarding him for another behavior, such as *sit* or *down*. If need be, offer the reward from the palm of your hand or drop it on the ground. Additionally, consider giving your dog a time-out for impolite grabs. Also practice teaching him to take food gently. For some dogs, it takes only a few intermittent reinforcements to trigger a resurgence of a shark-like behavior when taking food from your hands.

anticipate the next practice session. As your dog becomes more savvy and enthusiastic about the training game, longer sessions can be extended to thirty to forty minutes.

Opportunity Training

Controlled practice sessions are essential for teaching new behaviors, but training should also be incorporated into your dog's daily routine and activities. Throughout the day, use as many things as possible to reward your dog for desired behaviors. Use food, toys, attention, and access to the environment as leverage to reinforce behaviors you want. For example, ask your dog to *sit* and then hand target before you invite him on the couch. Additionally, take advantage of tiny training moments throughout the day. If you see your dog about to head to you, call him. If our dog is lying quietly while you eat your meal, calmly praise him.

TRAINER'S TIP

Variable Reinforcements

A slot machine dispenses payoffs randomly to keep gamblers playing and hoping for any reward, whether it be a small win or a jackpot. This also applies to training your dog. Once your dog understands a behavior, dispense variable rewards at random intervals so he will become highly motivated to continue to play the training game. For a well-trained dog with lots of experience, even tiny rewards like a piece of kibble or a little verbal praise is sufficient to maintain the behavior. From his point of view, you may reward him next time with steak or a vigorous game of tug. The only way to find out is to keep playing the game. Vary the rate of reward, but make sure those jackpots come once in a while. Otherwise, your dog may give up playing the game, like a gambler who has finally concluded that he or she will never win big.

The Foundation of Focus

Teaching your dog to reliably respond to your requests begins with successfully teaching him to give you his undivided attention on request. Some dogs do this readily when a person chooses to interact with them. For others, it takes a more concerted effort. Without your dog's focus and attention, lessons are wasted. Your canine student will be distracted by other matters.

Begin teaching your dog to be focused and engaged in your home. Gradually work up to more challenging environments, such as a public street or park.

Watch Me

Teaching your dog to make eye contact guarantees that he is focused on you. This is an excellent first step in setting the tone that training is about teamwork. As some dogs may perceive direct eye contact as potentially threatening—especially more cautious dogs—it may take some time for them to become comfortable with this idea. In addition to ensuring that you have your dog's attention, making eye contact also serves to build trust and confidence.

The "Watch Me" exercise is one of the easiest to master because there is little mechanical skill required. Yet it can be challenging to remain still, calm, and passive as you wait for your dog to *choose* to focus on you.

- To begin, keep your dog on leash to gently prevent him from roaming around to sniff and investigate.
- Stand still and wait for him to look at you. Mark and reward him when he does.
- If your dog doesn't look at you, simply wait. Don't reach for him or talk. He will eventually look at you to solicit attention or simply out of curiosity.
- As your dog more consistently focuses on you, hold a treat with your arm outstretched to your side. This makes the exercise more challenging. It is the first step in teaching your dog to focus on you in more distracting environments. In this case, in order to get the treat, he has to look away from it.
- Continue to add movement and distractions by placing food and toys nearby, but keep them far enough out of reach to prevent your dog from making contact with them until you give him permission to do so.
- Practice in other areas of your home, and then outdoors. Try to practice somewhere new each day, such as a driveway, a hallway, or in your neighbor's yard.
- In a highly distracting environment like a park, it may take some time for your dog to choose to focus on you and make eye contact. After practicing for a few days, he will focus more quickly and be able to concentrate for longer periods of time.

Target Training

Target training teaches your dog to touch an object, such as a hand or the end of a target stick, with his nose or paw. This can be used as the foundation for many behaviors including *walk nicely on leash, come when called,* and performing many tricks. Targeting exercises boost canine and human confidence and enthusiasm for the training game because they are extremely easy to master.

Hand Targeting

Hand targeting teaches your dog to touch his nose to the palm of your hand or extended finger.

- It's great for teaching your dog to *come when called* because he learns to happily approach you, and your hand gives him a specific target to head to rather than circling around you or playing a game of "catch me if you can."
- It's a good way to help your dog refocus when you are training him to walk nicely on leash.
- It provides your dog with an easy "say please" behavior to earn access to what he wants. Want to head into the dog run? Touch my hand and then I will open the gate. Want to retrieve a tossed toy? Touch my palm and then go get it! Touching the hand becomes a button that the dog can press to earn things he wants.
- It helps to facilitate positive social interactions, especially for shy or tentative dogs. This training helps dogs develop a positive association between people's outstretched hands and rewards.
- It helps prevent and resolve behavior problems such as resource guarding because it provides an easy way to calmly redirect your dog away from objects. He earns a reward and gains confidence.

Getting a Handle on Hand Targeting

- Be ready with your clicker or marker word and a variety of tiny treats.
- Present your hand approximately 6 inches (15.2 centimeters) away from your dog's nose. Most dogs will investigate by touching nose to hand. Accidental touches count. Mark and reward with a treat from your other hand. The hand holding the treat should be kept hidden behind your back to avoid distracting him.

- If your dog doesn't touch your hand, don't push it toward him. Simply move it a bit, touch it yourself, or remove it and present it again to encourage him to investigate.

- Repeat a few times. Most dogs make a quick connection between touching your hand, hearing the marker sound, and getting a reward. After a few trials, they will repeat when you present your hand again.
- When you are confident he will touch your hand when you hold it 6 inches (15.2 centimeters) away, move your hand a bit further away so he must travel to reach it. Some dogs immediately learn this challenge. Or, you may need to gradually increase the distance 1 inch (2.5 centimeters) at a time. Practice moving your hand on different sides of your dog, and practice the exercise in different areas of the home.
- Once your dog is reliably touching your hand from 12 inches (30.4 centimeters) away raise the bar by moving back and away from him so he must move a greater distance. This is where hand targeting shines as a foundation for teaching *come when called*.
- When your dog performs the exercise reliably, you are ready to add a verbal cue. Say the word *"Touch,"* just prior to presenting your hand.
- Begin adding the verbal cue in an environment with minimal distractions, and work at a close distance. This way, you can be certain your dog will successfully make the association between the word and the presentation of your hand (the visual cue).
- Practice outdoors in various environments and enlist family and friends to play hand targeting games.

Try the Target Stick

Teaching your dog to touch or target to a stick is helpful when teaching him to walk on leash or learn tricks like spin. You can purchase a target stick from a training supply company or make one from a wooden dowel with a bit of brightly colored tape on the tip. Follow the same instructions for hand targeting, but present your dog with the end of the stick rather than your hand. You can also have fun teaching your dog to target to objects like small containers, a cone, or a location.

Target to a Mat

Teaching your dog to settle on a mat is a useful skill for mealtimes. You can also bring a relaxation mat when you want your dog to rest calmly outside the home, such as at an outdoor café.

- Sit on the ground near the mat with your dog on leash.
- Wait for your dog to look at the mat or make any movement toward it, then mark and reward.
- If he steps toward the mat, mark and reward.
- Gradually increase your requirements for earning a treat. For example, only reward him if he

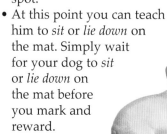

makes contact with the mat with one paw. Mark and reward him.
- You can ask your dog to hand target off the mat so he has another opportunity to practice going back to it.
- Next, try for two paws, and gradually mark and reward for all four paws on the mat.
- When your dog is reliably stepping onto the mat, move it to a slightly different spot.
- At this point you can teach him to *sit* or *lie down* on the mat. Simply wait for your dog to *sit* or *lie down* on the mat before you mark and reward.

- Gradually increase the length of time you expect him to stay on the mat. Release him by saying "*OK!*" or "*All done!*" and be sure to vary brief mat stays with longer stays.
- Work on standing up and/or walking gradually further away while your dog stays on the mat.
- Lastly, substitute a different location, towel, or bed so this becomes a flexible cue.

Sit

Sit is a supremely simple behavior that can greatly enrich your dog's life. If your dog will sit reliably on cue, you can ask him to do so to say hello politely, before going in and out of doorways, when moving forward on a walk or at street corners, or before allowing him to have access to furniture or laps. In these ways, your dog learns to use mannerly behavior in a variety of contexts, all thanks to learning to sit on cue.

Using the Capturing Method to Teach *Sit*

- With your dog on leash, stand or sit in front of him and show him a treat.
- Ignore any behavior other than sitting. When he sits, mark and reward.
- Take a step away and repeat.
- Within about five to ten repetitions, your dog will start to offer the *sit* more promptly.
- When you are confident your dog will *sit* when you show him the treat, say "*Sit*" just prior to doing so.
- Mark and reward.
- If your dog doesn't *sit*, simply turn away from him, count to five, and then try again. This way he learns that the game ends if he doesn't respond.

Using the Luring Method to Teach *Sit*

- Hold a treat between your thumb and forefinger at your dog's nose.
- Raise your hand up and back over your dog's head, between his ears, but not high enough to encourage jumping.
- As your dog's head tilts back, his rear will move in the other direction toward the floor (like a see-saw, where one end goes up and the other goes down).
- Mark and reward him when his rear hits the floor. It is better to mark a bit earlier than later! Offer the treat from your hand or toss it to the floor.

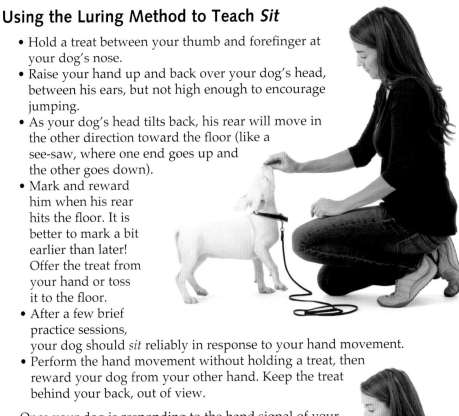

- After a few brief practice sessions, your dog should *sit* reliably in response to your hand movement.
- Perform the hand movement without holding a treat, then reward your dog from your other hand. Keep the treat behind your back, out of view.

Once your dog is responding to the hand signal of your raised hand without the treat, add your verbal cue right before your hand begins to move. Dogs learn by association. With repetition, your dog will learn to associate the word *"sit"* with the behavior of putting his rear on the floor and earning the reward.

- Practice with the rewards in your treat pouch or pocket.
- Practice with the treat on a nearby counter or held by a training partner.
- Practice saying *"Sit"* without any hand movement or treats nearby.

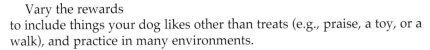

Vary the rewards to include things your dog likes other than treats (e.g., praise, a toy, or a walk), and practice in many environments.

Down

Down is a useful skill for times when you want your dog to remain in a position for prolonged periods, such as staying on his mat while you eat your meal. Learning to lie down on request for prolonged periods also helps your dog learn to relax. However, many dogs feel more vulnerable when lying down, so they may not learn this concept as quickly as *sit*.

Using the Capturing Method to Teach *Down*

Begin teaching this with your dog in a location where he is likely to lie down comfortably, such as on carpeting or a dog bed. Avoid looking directly in your dog's eyes. This may encourage him to stand and maintain eye contact.

- Wait for him to *lie down*, and mark and reward.
- Repeat.
- When you are confident your dog is just about to *lie down*, say "Down" the moment before he does. Mark and reward.
- Practice this exercise in various environments, and be prepared to ask your dog to *lie down* whenever you see him just about to do so and reward him.

Using the Luring Method to Teach *Down*

- Use a lure to get your dog to *sit*.
- Hold a small treat between your thumb and forefinger with your palm facing down, near your dog's nose.
- Move your hand toward your dog's chest, between his front feet and toward the floor.

- Most dogs will lower their heads to follow the lure and naturally begin to slide to a *down* position.
- As soon as his belly touches the floor, mark and give a treat.

- If he has difficulty with the *down*, break it into steps. Mark and reward him when he lowers his head slightly.
- Mark and reward him for his gradually lower body position each step of the way.
- Teach him to associate a visual clue with *down* by following the same steps as *sit*. With your hand, make a sweeping gesture toward the floor. When he has learned to respond to this gesture, you can add your verbal cue to the exercise.
- You should also practice luring your dog from a *stand* to a *down*. When your dog is standing, lower your hand to the floor and slightly toward his chest so your dog slides back into a *down* position.

Stand

This has many practical applications, such as when you want your dog to stand still for grooming or a veterinary exam.

Using the Capturing Method to Teach *Stand*

- Wait for your dog to stand still, and mark and reward.
- Repeat until you can predict when your dog will stand up. At that point, begin to say "*Stand*" just prior to when he does it.
- Practice in various environments.

Using the Luring Method to Teach *Stand*

- Have your dog go into a *sit* or *down* position.
- Hold a treat in front of your dog's nose and move your hand forward and away, to where his nose will be when he stands.
- Mark and reward when he follows the lure into a standing position.
- When you are confident he will follow your hand, add the verbal cue just prior to doing so.

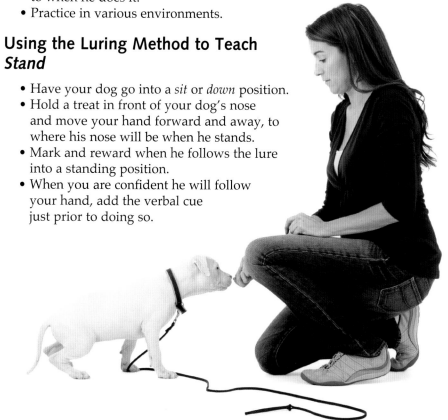

Puppy Push Ups

Puppy push-ups are an excellent way for your dog to practice these individual behaviors and learn to discriminate the cues for *sit, down,* and *stand.*

- Cue or lure your dog to *sit,* then mark and reward.
- Cue or lure your dog to *down,* then mark and reward.
- Reverse these two exercises by practicing from *down,* and back up to *sit.* Mark and reward each step of the *sit, down,* and *sit* sequence.

- Practice one full push-up (*sit* to *down* to *sit*) for one mark and reward. Practice a push-up and add a *stand* at the end; then mark and reward at the end of sequence.
- Mix up the sequence of positions and begin to mark and reward your dog variably.

Stay

Sit, down, and *stand* become exponentially more valuable once your dog learns to stay in the requested position until he is released. *Stay* teaches your dog to try longer and harder to get a reward.

Three general components affect the degree of challenge in this exercise.

1. The distance between you and your dog
2. The duration of time you expect your dog to remain stationary.
3. The distractions in the environment.

Working on impulse control exercises is recommended prior to working on a formal *stay* (see Chapter 8).

- Ask your dog to go into a *sit* or *down* position.

- Count to three before you mark and reward him for remaining in position.
- Repeat.
- After your dog responds to your *sit* or *down* cue, gradually increase the pause to five seconds, then seven, then ten and so on.
- Vary the length of time you wait before marking his response from three to ten or more seconds.

- If your dog gets up before the mark try again, but make things a little easier by shortening the time before you mark. The fact that he didn't get the reward gives him an opportunity to learn that breaking a *stay* doesn't work.
- When your dog will *stay* for twenty to thirty seconds, add some distance by taking half a step away. Decrease the duration of the *stay* when you do this.
- Gradually increase the distance you walk away.

- Offer calm, quiet verbal praise as encouragement to keep your dog in place as you extend the *stay*.
- When working on distance, always step closer to your dog before the release; this will decrease your dog's eagerness to be released and run to you.

- Begin to add minor distractions to the exercise, but decrease the duration and distance.
- Gradually add varying components of duration, distance, and distraction to the challenge. For instance, have a friend or family member do something to distract your dog as you stay closer to reinforce his *stay*.
- If your dog consistently breaks the *stay*, he is being asked to do something he does not yet understand. Backtrack a few steps and work on strengthening his understanding of the concept.

Walking Nicely on Leash

Whether a dog is 5 or 150 pounds, few things will enhance his life as much as regular walks. Walking is an outlet for physical energy, but it also provides an opportunity for your dog to be mentally stimulated by countless sights, sounds, smells, people, and experiences. Additionally, walking your dog will provide the same benefits for you.

If your dog is not familiar with wearing a collar and leash, especially if he is a young pup, help him adjust to them indoors before taking him for walks. While he is wearing the collar and leash, give him some tasty treats and let him play with a food-stuffed toy while you supervise. Start introducing the concept of walking on leash indoors, where your dog will encounter fewer enticing distractions.

You must first establish your concept of acceptable leash manners before you can teach this to your dog. Walking nicely on leash is often called "heeling," but that is actually a term more accurately attributed to competitive obedience. Dogs are required to walk on the handler's left side with their ear lined up with the seam of the handler's pants. In daily life, most of us are satisfied with a more casual version of this. Walking calmly on a loose leash without lagging, lunging, or crossing back and forth in front of you generally qualifies as fine leash manners.

Teaching your dog to walk nicely on leash is incredibly simple.

- Ignore any unwanted pulling by stopping and standing still when it happens.
- Praise and reward your dog when he keeps his leash slack while walking.

Why Dogs Pull

A young pup is likely to remain close by your side because he does not yet possess the confidence to wander away and explore unfamiliar settings. As he matures and becomes more confident, his investigative nature flourishes.

Dogs pull on leash because they are curious to investigate their environments; each step brings them in contact with new and interesting smells, sights, and sounds. A habit of pulling on the leash often starts by allowing your dog to pull toward a hydrant or bush, in the hope that he will choose it as a potty spot. Unfortunately, the dog learns pulling on leash is the best way to get where he wants to go. Regardless of your dog's age, do not reward pulling.

Bad leash manners are also the result of poor impulse control and not adhering to a "Learn to Earn" program (see Chapter Two). Dogs that haven't learned to walk nicely on leash may be walked less frequently, for shorter durations, and/or in a more restrained manner. All of these factors contribute to the dog's pent-up energy, frustration, and stress, which does not bode well for learning better leash manners. It becomes a vicious cycle. Frequent, intense pulling on leash may also exacerbate tendencies toward leash aggression.

- A loose leash is like a gas pedal, which results in the reward of moving forward; a tight leash is like the brake, which removes your dog's reward of moving forward.
- Make walks fun by frequently changing direction and pace.

Start Indoors

Like any successful team, you need to practice at the home game (indoors) prior to the away game (outdoors). If your dog doesn't follow you on a slack leash in a less distracting indoor environment, he will surely pull on the leash when he is outdoors. Your dog needs plenty of opportunities to practice walking nicely in a controlled setting. For instance, teach him to walk past a treat on the floor at home before expecting him to ignore a chicken bone he finds on the street during a walk. Likewise, you need opportunities to practice standing still when the leash pulls taut, and rewarding your dog by moving along when it is slack. Accurately timed feedback plays a crucial role in his ability to master this concept.

- Schedule practice sessions just prior to your dog's mealtime.
- Stand still. Mark and reward your dog for looking at you.

- Say *"Let's go"* or make a little kissing noise and take a few steps forward.
- If the leash remains slack, mark and reward. If the leash tightens, stop and say nothing. Try again by taking a few steps in the opposite direction.
- Repeat. Don't wait long in between repetitions, or your dog may become deeply engrossed in a distraction.
- You can also use a lure (a piece of food in your hand to encourage your dog to follow at your side) or a target (the palm of your hand or a target stick).
- Gradually increase the number of steps you take between marking and rewarding your dog for a slack leash.
- Practice in other areas of the house.
- Start practicing without a lure in your hand. Keep rewards for walking with a slack leash in your pocket or treat pouch.

Add Mild Distractions

- Practice walking toward a mildly interesting object in the house, such as a toy placed about 10 to 15 feet (3 to 4.6 meters) away on the floor.
- When the leash is slack, stop about 2 feet (0.6 meters) from the toy and wait for your dog to sit. Mark, reward, and release him to play with the toy.
- If your dog pulls, stop and back away.
- Repeat.

Add More Challenging Distractions Indoors

- Place a jar of treats or a favorite toy about 10 to 15 feet (3 to 4.6 meters) away from your dog.
- Start walking your dog toward it.
- If your dog pulls, turn and walk back to where you came from.
- Head toward the toy again and ask your dog to sit when you are a foot away from it. Then tell him, *"OK! Go get it!"*
- This can make for a slow walk, but it's worth it!

DANGER!

If your dog rushes forward, grabs and tugs at the leash, or seems to tune you out completely, he may be over-aroused or stressed. This state of mind precludes learning. Practice in less distracting environments and work on the impulse-control exercises discussed in Chapter Eight.

Do not try to stop your dog or reprimand him by yanking on his leash. This can injure his neck or back and encourage insensitivity to touch.

Consider using a front-clip harness or head halter for gentle leverage to prevent your dog from pulling. Retractable leashes are not recommended if you want your dog to walk nicely on leash. They are designed to be taut at all times. As a result, your dog will become desensitized to the discomfort of a tight leash and will inevitably pull more.

Going Outside

When your dog is doing well with his leash training in the house, begin using a variable rate of reinforcement by varying the number of steps he takes on a slack leash before rewarding him. Begin practicing in hallways if you live in an apartment building, or your driveway. Use a higher rate of reinforcement when making this transition.

Typically, dogs become increasingly distracted and aroused as a walk progresses. So, increase the rate, value, and variety of rewards to adequately compete with your dog's state of distraction and arousal. Rewards for walking nicely for a few steps might include an opportunity for an extra-long sniff at a hydrant.

If your dog is a social butterfly, you need to be extra vigilant to prevent him from becoming overly excited or distracted by potential social encounters when you are practicing outdoors. If someone approaches, let that person know your dog is learning good leash manners and you would appreciate his or her cooperation.

Walks should not consist of a long, straight, and inevitably boring route. Provide your dog with a more enriching experience. Vary the direction, destination, and pace, and occasionally change direction and practice exercises like *sit*, *down*, and hand targets. Practice backing away from your dog and calling him toward you during a walk. This will encourage him to pay attention while walking by your side and to *come when called*. This unpredictability encourages your dog to pay greater attention to you because he won't be able to anticipate your next step. This in turn gives you far more opportunities to reward his good behavior. Essentially, it comes down to making yourself more interesting than a squirrel or another passing dog.

Stage outdoor distractions, such as a friend walking by with shopping bags, a calm dog on leash, or someone on a skateboard or bike. However, some distractions should generally be avoided, such as a group of rowdy kids. Begin working at a distance, at a moderate pace that makes it easier for your dog to walk with a slack leash. Gradually move closer to the distractions as your dog's leash manners improve.

If your dog is a backpeddler, lagging behind, or putting on the breaks, he may be experiencing pain due to a medical issue, or fear due to inadequate socialization.

If you have ruled out both, he may simply need more time to learn the concept of walking on leash. Be patient. When he lags or stops, stop, look forward, and wait. When you feel slack on the leash, which may take a minute or more, mark and reward him. Do not make eye contact or encourage him when he lags. This will help him understand that the good stuff goes away when he stops or lags, and that moving forward with you makes good stuff happen.

Come When Called

Teaching your dog to *come when called* is like an insurance policy that could one day save his life. With any insurance policy, you must make an initial agreement and pay the premiums. In this case, teaching your dog the behavior becomes the initial agreement. Pay the premiums by practicing and rewarding him regularly. Every skill needs to be maintained through continued variable reinforcement. This is particularly true for *come when called*.

Prevention is the best medicine. Plenty of daily practice will pay off because you won't have to spend time on remedial training later on.

If your dog doesn't reliably *come when called*, you will most likely live in constant fear that he might break free of his leash or dash out the front door and meet with disaster. A dog that *comes when called* can enjoy much more freedom because his safety is best ensured.

Two mitigating factors can interfere with your dog's response to coming when called:

- The relationship your dog has with his family
- The mechanics of the behavior

Ultimately, you want your dog to choose to come back to you even when he is faced with things he finds more interesting. You can enhance your dog's level of cooperation by implementing a "Learn to Earn" program (see page 34). Regularly practice focus and name recognition exercises, as well as hand targeting, *sit, down*, and *stand*.

DANGER!

When first teaching the basics of a recall, be careful not to put your dog in a situation where his lack of skills could endanger his life or give him an opportunity to practice uncooperative behavior.

Many people fail to adequately train their dogs to *come when called*. If their dogs come at all, they often use the opportunity to play "keep away" when someone reaches for their collar. Teach your dog to love having his collar grabbed by playing the "*Gotcha!*" game. Briefly and gently grab his collar and reward him. Practice this many times each day. Begin practicing indoors, and gradually introduce him to forceful grabs. This way, he will not become frightened if he is handled this way in an emergency.

If your dog gets loose and won't come back when called, do not yell or chase after him. Most dogs will run farther away due to fear of punishment or a desire to play a game of chase. Switch tactics. Happily encourage your dog and run in the opposite direction, or kneel down and pretend to investigate something that may entice him to head in your direction.

During this training, a long leash will provide your dog with plenty of room to roam and a safe backup tool during outdoor training sessions. When appropriate, you can drop the line of about 20 to 30 feet (6.1 to 9.1 meters), but be prepared to step on it in order to stop your dog when necessary. Tying a few knots along the length of the leash approximately 2 feet (0.6 meter) apart will prevent it from slipping when you step on it.

Your dog's readiness for off-leash privileges will vary from day to day and even moment to moment. Behavior is constantly changing. On some days and in certain situations, your dog will be more reliable. The better you understand your dog, the better equipped you will be to gauge his need for management while he learns to reliably respond to your requests.

Even when they are well trained to *come when called,* most dogs have a critical distance at which they become likely to *come when called*. Make sure you identify your dog's critical distance, which can vary depending on the environment. Only allow your dog to range at a reasonable and safe distance.

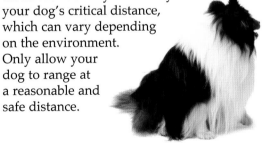

Choose and Use Your Cue with Care

Choose a distinctive cue word that is reserved only for this exercise. This will ensure that it effectively sends the message that coming back to you will result in a high-value reward for your dog. Do not use this word in any other context. That can muddy the meaning, because there is a chance your dog will learn to associate it with something he does not find highly rewarding. That includes potentially unpleasant experiences. If your dog tries evasive maneuvers when it's time for a bath or nail trimming, approach him calmly, offer a tasty treat, snap on his leash, and walk him to the bath or grooming table.

Hide-and-Seek

Play hide-and-seek indoors or in a safely enclosed outdoor area. Encourage your dog to watch you and quickly orient to your direction, even when you are out of sight.

Enlist the assistance of another person to hold your dog while you hide close by. If you don't have a helper, place a few pieces of your dog's food on the ground to distract him while you hide.

TRAINING TRUTH

Dealing with Distractions

Be creative when scouting new, safe locations to practice outdoors. Start with environments that are less challenging, such as apartment lobbies and hallways, friend's homes and yards, recreation centers, and parks.

When adding distractions, especially those that are more challenging for your dog, be sure to adjust the distance and the duration of the exercise accordingly. Make one aspect of the exercise less challenging when another becomes more so. Gradually work toward making two parts of the exercise equally challenging until you can eventually work on all three components at once.

- Toss a food treat about 10 feet (3 meters) away from you.
- When your dog has finished the treat, call him to you.
- Have your helper place a low-value toy a few feet outside your dog's return path and stand near it. The helper should be prepared to pick it up or step on it if your dog doesn't head to you.
- Repeat in different locations.
- Practice calling your dog away from something he is highly interested in, such as a piece of a hot dog.
- If he doesn't *come*, for several repetitions call him away from something less distracting in order to set him up to succeed.

- Call your dog and reward him with praise and a food or toy reward when he finds you.
- At an advanced level you can make the game more challenging by hiding further away so your dog must also use his sense of smell to find you.

Restrained Recall (to Build Speed and Enthusiasm)

- Have someone hold your dog gently by his collar.
- Show him a treat and move 5 to 10 feet (1.5 to 3 meters) away.
- Call and encourage him as he heads to you, and reward when he arrives.
- Repeat.
- Practice in various areas of your home and at greater distances.

Toss and Call

This is one of the easiest ways to reinforce a recall. Set aside at least ten pieces of your dog's dry food to play this game each day.

- Toss one piece of food about 5 to 10 feet (1.5 to 3 meters) away from you.
- The moment he finishes eating the food, encourage him to come back to you with a kiss noise or by presenting your hand for him to target.
- Mark and reward every time he comes back to you.
- Repeat in various rooms.

Ping-Pong Recall

This game can be played with two or more people. They should be approximately 5 feet (1.5 meters) away from each other to begin.
- One person makes a kiss noise to get the dog's attention and extends a hand for him to target. The others ignore the dog (no eye contact, talking, or petting) so he can easily make the right choice.
- Mark when he approaches the right person and touches their hand. Reward him and then hide your hands behind your back.
- Repeat with the next person.

Reserve the best rewards for the most distracting situations. Once you are able to call your dog away from high-level distractions, like a play session or a sniffy spot, reward him with treats for returning to you, and send him off to play again. This way, he earns a jackpot reward of a food treat and a life reward.

Impulse Control

Good Things Come to Those Who Are Patient

One of the many wonderful things about dogs is their ability to live fully in the moment. They generally investigate new things with enthusiasm. Their outlook on life can best be summed up as: Why put anything off until later when you can enjoy it right now? Like many canine qualities, this enthusiasm to take advantage of each moment can be both beneficial and detrimental to their joy and safety. A dog that approaches happily to greet us when we arrive home from a long day is appreciated. But, we rarely appreciate a level of excitement that causes the dog to dash out the front door or jump around wildly, knocking us over.

Impulse control is the ability to respond calmly and thoughtfully to stimuli. It is the result of developing default manners and patience instead of a *"Do it now!"* attitude. For example, a dog that refrains from grabbing food off the coffee table displays a great deal of impulse control. Without training, this dog would probably grab the food.

All social creatures must learn self-control. In the wild, impulse control becomes a matter of survival. For example, if a wild dog impulsively chases an animal instead of using a hunting strategy, he would probably lose the opportunity for a meal. Likewise, impulsively chasing a skunk or porcupine would lead to very unpleasant consequences. In the wild, animals learn self-control through a combination of maturity and trial and error. Unfortunately, those that fail to learn this skill don't survive.

In a domestic setting, a lack of impulse control may result in equally dire consequences. Aside from the primary concern of safety, poor self-control adds stress and frustration to the canine-human relationship. Dogs lacking impulse control require much more of our time to control them, keep them safe, and guide them toward mannerly behavior. Many behavior problems, including excessive barking, jumping on people, chasing moving objects, counter surfing and pulling on a leash, result from a lack of adequate self-control. Consequentially, the dog may be banished from enriching social interactions with family and friends, or even surrendered to a shelter due to what is deemed "incorrigible" behavior.

Management to Support Self-Control Success

Each dog has unique triggers for arousal. Some have a low arousal threshold, while others have more innate self-control. But, even dogs with good self-control are often put to the test in a busy household, where they are constantly bombarded by challenging activities and stimuli.

Dogs may also be inadvertently conditioned to be active and impulsive. A common mistake is giving the dog too much freedom in the house. Some people feel that it's unkind to restrict the dog's freedom, or they assume that constant activity will eventually tire the dog.

This plan usually ends in disaster. Constant activity elevates the dog's level of arousal and excitement, which results in more jumping, barking, whining, and chewing. The dog's ability to use self-control also deteriorates. In this situation, the dog can be compared to an overtired, overstimulated child. Management is the best way to help your dog learn to settle until his impulse control capabilities are strong (see "Tools to Have in Your Trainer's Toolbox" on page 55.)

PAWS TO CONSIDER

A mannerly dog should understand behaviors such as *sit*, *down*, and *come*, but the underlying concept is teaching your dog to exhibit self control. This can be challenging, especially in potentially exciting situations. A dog with good self-control is likely to have much more freedom because it is easier to get his attention and gain his cooperation.

Dogs are experts at teaching each other self-control. Puppies are given a lot of leeway by well-socialized adult dogs—they are allowed to pounce, grab, nip, pull, and sometimes even take valued items, such as bones. But, as the pup nears adolescence, their "puppy license" expires and adult dogs expect them to exhibit more considerate behavior. A gradual progression toward good self-control is equally important for a dog's interaction with people. In this area, dogs are naturally far better teachers than humans. But, it is our responsibility to teach our dogs to exhibit self-control so that they can successfully live side by side with us. Therefore, it is our responsibility to learn how to teach them as effectively and humanely as possible.

Instilling Impulse Control

Technically, all training exercises serve as impulse control exercises. Having your dog *sit* while you fix his meal or attach his leash are simple, quick ways to practice impulse control. The following exercises are designed to help your dog develop the emotional and physical skills necessary for self-control in his daily life.

Self-Control Exercises

Self-control exercises must be practiced in many different situations in order for your dog to generalize this concept. In certain situations, it will be harder for him to exhibit self-control. Sitting and waiting politely for dinner in your kitchen is probably much easier for your dog than doing this at the entrance of a dog park. Recognize the varying challenges and provide your dog with many opportunities to practice in different settings. Eventually, he will be able to display polite behavior in almost any environment.

Automatic *Sit* Approaches

Teaching your dog to *sit* automatically (without a verbal or hand cue) when people approach is an ideal exercise to instill a foundation for self-control. The objective is to help your dog understand that remaining calm is the best way to earn positive social interaction.

If you prefer to have your dog *stand* (with four paws on the ground) for greetings, simply follow these steps and replace the *sit* with *stand*.

- Use a leash to tether your dog to a stable object just prior to mealtime.
- Step 6 feet (1.8 meters) away from your dog.
- From this distance, wait for your dog to *sit*. Do not approach your dog until he offers a polite *sit* without instruction from you.
- The moment he does, mark (using a clicker or by saying "*Yes*"), approach, and reward him.
- If he jumps up, take a few steps back and wait for him to *sit* again.
- Repeat until you are able to make contact with your dog, calmly pet him, and reward for sitting as opposed to jumping.

Practice this exercise with your dog tethered in various locations around the house. Employ the same technique when your dog is in his crate, exercise pen, or behind a baby gate. Once your dog understands this concept, enlist friends to practice this exercise with him.

With plenty of practice, your dog will learn that people approach in response to polite sitting—not rambunctious jumping.

Take Food Gently

Most dogs are tempted by food and toys held in a person's hand, and they will impulsively grab these things without permission. Teach your dog that he will only receive food from your hands if he patiently waits until it is offered and takes it gently.

BETTER BEHAVIOR

Set a good example when teaching your dog to have impulse control. Communicating to him in harsh, sharp, excited, demanding tones and gestures will increase his level of stress and arousal. Calm and thoughtful behavior on your part sends a clear message and makes it easier for your dog to follow suit.

- Tether your dog to a stable object.
- Hold a low-value treat between your index finger and thumb.
- Offer the treat to your dog. If you feel teeth on your skin, remove your hand before he can take the treat.
- Offer the food again. When your dog shows even the slightest bit of inhibition in the way he takes the food (e.g., you feel less pain or he licks the food), mark and reward.
- Gradually raise your expectations by marking and rewarding your dog only when he takes the treat ever more gently.
- In future sessions, repeat the exercise using higher value treats in different areas of your home, when your dog is not tethered. When you are outdoors, practice having him take treats from other people.

Leave It

Teaching your dog to refrain from touching certain food, toys, and other objects can be extremely useful in many situations. For instance, it will prevent him from picking up a pill you drop on the floor, a chicken bone on the street, or your neighbor's groceries in the elevator.

Begin teaching this concept in a calm environment when your dog is relaxed. Use a lower value treat, such as a piece of dry dog food, for the *leave it* item. As your dog masters the game gradually increase the value of the *leave it* item.

If your dog is more enthusiastic, tether him to a stable object so he can't jump on you and you can easily move the *leave it* item out of his reach.

Leave It in Hand

- Begin with ten to twenty treats in your pouch for each session.
- Hold a low-value piece of food in your closed hand about 6 inches (15.2 centimeters) from your dog's nose.
- Keep your hand closed as your dog sniffs and licks it.
- When he backs off (even half an inch), mark and reward with the treat.
- Repeat the mark and reward for increased periods of patience.

- When he consistently stops trying to get the treat from your hand, begin to open your hand a little bit, and close your hand if he tries to take the food.
- When he refrains from taking the food from your slightly open hand, mark and reward.
- When you can present your open hand and your dog waits patiently for five seconds, you can then add a cue because you are confident the behavior will happen. Say *"Leave it"* just prior to presenting your hand. Mark and reward if he pauses briefly for one or two seconds.
- Move your hand closer and vary the length of time he must wait for you to mark and reward, and/or wait for eye contact so he learns to look at you to get what he wants.
- Practice in various environments and have other people try this exercise with him.

Leave It on the Ground

Start with your dog on leash, or tether him so you can easily step away and give him a time-out if necessary. Use a low-value food treat for the item you want your dog to ignore on request, and a higher value, soft (easily consumed) treat as a reward.

Step 1:

- Place the low-value treat on the ground approximately 1 foot (0.3 meter) from your dog.
- If your dog steps toward it, pick it up or cover it with your hand.
- If he pauses for a second, mark, uncover your hand, and pick up the treat and offer it to him, or give him a higher value treat from your other hand.

DANGER!

You may be undermining your dog's impulse control if:

- you continue to prepare his meal while he jumps around;
- you continue to approach his crate, ex-pen, or tether spot while he jumps;
- you push him off when he jumps; or
- you make eye contact or talk to him when he barks or whines.

These are examples of rewarding a dog's impulsive behavior with your touch, your voice, and your attention. Remember, behavior that is rewarded is more likely to occur in the future. When the rewards cease, in time so will the behavior.

- Repeat and gradually extend the time to a five-second pause prior to marking and rewarding.
- When he consistently waits for five seconds, add the cue *"Leave it"* just prior to placing the treat on the ground.
- Repeat and gradually build up to a ten-second pause prior to marking and rewarding.

Step 2:

When your dog reaches the point where he has reliable self-control for ten seconds, begin adding challenges to the exercise, one at a time. Make part of the exercise more challenging, such as decreasing the distance between your dog and the treat. Balance this by making another part less challenging. For example, bring the treat closer to your dog, but decrease the duration of the expected pause prior to the mark and treat. Then gradually begin extending the time again.

Challenges that can be added to this exercise include:

- Moving the treat closer to your dog
- Waiting longer before marking and rewarding
- Practicing while you sit in a chair
- Working toward gradually standing up
- Gradually stepping farther away from the treat
- Dropping the treat in front of your dog rather than placing it there
- Practicing in different areas of your home
- Practicing in more realistic situations, such as placing the treat on a coffee table.

Treat, Bowl, or Toy Overhead

This exercise will teach your dog that he should not jump up to snatch things from people's hands. It will teach your dog that he should never snatch things from people's hands. (It may seem like teasing, but real teasing never results in so many rewards.)

Step 1:

- Begin with your dog tethered to a stable object.
- Hold a treat approximately 1 foot (0.3 meter) above your dog's head and ask him to *sit* (or *stand*).
- When he is sitting, begin lowering the treat in your hand.
- Do this fairly quickly, because doing it slowly creates more of a temptation and challenge for him.
- As long as he remains sitting, keep moving the treat down to his mouth.
- If he jumps up and tries to snatch it, pull your hand back up.
- The instant he *sits*, lower your hand back down.
- Imagine your dog's rear end is controlling a string attached to your hand. When it rises off the ground, your hand simultaneously goes up. The timelier your response, the more quickly your dog will learn.
- With repetitions he will realize that remaining in a sitting position will make the treat move all the way to his mouth!
- When he understands the exercise, move your hand slower to make it more challenging.

Step 2:

- Repeat the exercise using treats, toys, food, and a water bowl.
- Hold the item while standing, and wait for your dog to sit.
- Once he is seated, begin to lower it to the floor.

- If he gets up, raise the item out of his reach. Do this silently, without verbal instruction or reprimands. This way, your dog has an opportunity to figure out that his behavior impacts his access to things he wants. This makes the experience more meaningful.
- This lesson may take a while. Start working on it when you have plenty of time and patience.

Step 3:

You can also use this exercise to improve your dog's leash manners.

- Place an empty bowl on the ground. Attach your dog's leash and walk him past the bowl, keeping it out of his reach.
- If he pulls at the leash and tries to reach the bowl, stop and wait.
- The instant he looks at you, mark and reward him with a high-value reward.
- Repeat the exercise until he automatically looks at you when you pass the bowl.
- Now place a low-value treat in the bowl and repeat the exercise. As his self-control improves, begin to place more appealing treats in the bowl.
- Practicing this exercise outdoors will encourage your dog to pay attention to you during walks when he passes something tempting, such as garbage on the street.

BETTER BEHAVIOR

Biscuit on Paw

An advanced challenge for *leave it* is teaching your dog to lie down and ignore a biscuit placed on his front paw. Start by placing it about 2 inches (5 centimeters) from his paw, and mark and reward him when he leaves it alone. Gradually move the biscuit closer until you can place it directly on his paw. This not only improves his impulse control; it also helps dogs overcome paw sensitivity. If your dog seems reluctant to have his paws touched, see page 105 for exercises to address this problem.

Impulse Control for Leash Manners

For many dogs, self-control becomes especially challenging during one of the highlights of their day—going for a walk. These exercises are specifically designed to teach impulse control during walks. Teach your dog to show restraint beginning with the first part of a walk, having his leash attached to his collar.

Step 1:

- Schedule practice sessions after your dog has had a potty break (i.e., when your dog is empty).
- Show your dog the leash and wait for him to *sit* or *stand* (as opposed to jumping).
- Once he *sits*, or remains standing, start to bring the leash down toward his collar. If your dog jumps, raise the leash away from his collar.
- When he *sits* or *stands* again, lower the leash toward his collar once more.

- Repeat until he *sits* or *stands* patiently while the leash is clipped to his collar, and offer a reward.

Step 2:
- Have your dog on leash indoors.
- Show him a low-value treat and toss it forward.
- He is likely to pull toward the treat. Stand still.
- When the leash is slack, mark and reward him with a treat from your hand.
- Turn to head in another direction and repeat steps 1 through 3.
- Gradually raise the challenge by waiting until his leash is slack and he looks at you before marking and rewarding him.
- Gradually step closer to the treat, and mark and reward when his leash remains slack.
- Practice this exercise outdoors.

BETTER BEHAVIOR

This skill can also be used to improve the reliability of your dog's recall:
- Gently toss a treat 10 or more feet (3 or more meters) away.
- With your dog on leash, call him to you in the opposite direction of the treat. Use the leash to gently prevent him from going toward the treat on the ground.
- When your dog heads toward you, mark and reward him with a treat that is higher in value than the one you tossed to the ground.

Step 3: Step, Stop, Sit

A walk can include many opportunities to practice impulse control.

- Take a step or two forward, stop, and wait for your dog to *sit*. Mark and reward.
- If the leash tightens, stop, stand still, and wait for him to *sit* or make eye contact with you before marking and stepping forward as a reward.
- This is a good way to encourage the habit of walking with a slack leash, especially if you practice both indoors and outdoors.
- You can reward him for walking on a slack leash and controlling his impulse to forge ahead with a treat or a few extra moments to sniff and investigate an interesting spot. This way, outdoor distractions can be used as valuable rewards.

Impulse Control Exit Strategies

Teaching your dog to automatically wait at doorways or when exiting his crate is a superb way to begin his walk with a brief but vital display of impulse control. If your dog customarily pushes his way out of his enclosure or drags you out of the front door, he is likely to continue imitating a sled dog all the way around the block. This lesson is also an important safety measure. It minimizes the possibility that your dog will leap out of a car or dash through a doorway into traffic. Ideally, your dog will *sit* or *stand* at doorways when the door is wide open, until he receives permission to walk through. Even when your dog does this reliably, you should always take precautions when you're with him by an open door.

TRAINER'S TIP

If you want your dog to exhibit self-control, be sure to set a good example. Harsh, sharp, excited, and demanding tones and gestures will cause your dog to become stressed and aroused. Calm and thoughtful behavior on your part sends a clear message and makes it easier for your dog to follow suit.

Crate Exit Etiquette

Your dog should learn to exit his crate calmly upon your signal. A dog that lunges out of a crate or other enclosure is being reinforced for lack of self-control, and this may encourage a similarly pushy approach in other situations, such as household doorways. Plan practice sessions just after a walk so your dog doesn't need a potty break.

- Place your dog in his crate. Sit in front of it and slightly to the side that opens.

- When he has four paws on the ground (that is, no pawing at the door), reach for the door latch.
- If he touches or pushes the door with nose or paw, remove your hand.
- When his four paws are again on the ground, reach for the door latch again.

- Repeat until you can open the door slightly.
- His reward for keeping four paws on the floor is the door continuing to be opened. The consequence of a lack of self-control is you don't open the door.
- Gradually open the door further. If your dog tries to push out of the crate, gently close the door, being careful not to startle him in the process. If he shows self-control say *"Okay"* so he can exit the crate.

Down with Doorway Dashing

- Schedule practice sessions after a potty break, and just before your dog's mealtime.
- Have your dog on leash and have tasty treats on hand.
- Begin practicing this exercise at doorways that your dog finds less interesting than the front door.
- Approach the door, stop and wait for your dog to *sit*. You can assist your dog by reminding him to *sit*, but the lesson will have a bigger impact if you allow him to figure this out on his own. This will also produce a more reliable response, which will become his default behavior at doorways.
- In your first session, your dog is likely to experiment with a number of behaviors in an effort to get what he wants (you to open the door). He may jump or bark. Ignore him until he *sits*, then mark and reward him.

- Repeat until he offers a *sit* as soon as he approaches the door. This indicates that he has had a light bulb moment and discovered for himself that sitting is the only rewarding option in this situation.

Step 2:
- Now try reaching for the door handle while your dog is sitting, before marking and rewarding him.
- If he gets up, remove your hand from the door handle and wait for him to *sit* again.
- When he can remain sitting while you touch the handle, mark and reward him.
- Repeat until he calmly remains sitting as you hold the handle.

Step 3:
Practice opening the door slightly and repeat the above steps. When he gets to the point where you can open the door fully and count to five, release him from the *sit* and walk him through the doorway as a reward.

Impulse Control as Part of Play

We should provide our dogs with plenty of appropriate outlets for their physical energy, but moments of "on" (excited behavior) must be balanced with equal moments of "off" (calm behavior).

If your dog is allowed to get into a highly excited state where he is unable to focus and respond to your requests, your time together will be less enjoyable.

A dog with self-control can be exuberant and playful, and at the same time able to focus on you and your requests. This is especially valuable in potentially high-excitement situations, such as playing with children. Helping your dog to cultivate this skill will make him better equipped to handle all sorts of potentially exciting situations. If necessary, he will be able to focus on you, despite competing attractions like food or another dog on a walk.

"Chill-Out" Game

Because it is so highly prized by so many dogs, play can be an especially important reward when teaching impulse control. The "chill-out" game superbly uses play as leverage. Allowing your dog to engage in long play sessions may result in a tired and calm dog in the short run. In the long run, long play sessions may potentially reinforce a state of arousal, making your dog less responsive to your requests. By sporadically interrupting his play with periods of calm, you can provide plenty of opportunities for him to understand that calmness may earn another play session as a reward. During these calm moments, your dog is also using up mental energy while working to maintain great self-control.

The ultimate goal of this game is to instill the ability to switch from a state of high-play arousal to a state of calm on request. This is accomplished by deliberately getting your dog into an excited state (beginning with a relatively low level of excitement and gradually increasing this throughout many practice sessions) in a controllable environment (e.g., your home or yard). This will improve your dog's self-control and teach him to respond to your requests in real-life situations when he is likely to be excited, such as when he visits the dog park or greets visitors.

Keep sessions brief, no longer than three to five minutes at first.

- Have your dog on leash and initiate play, beginning with very brief periods of low-level play. You want to anticipate "turning his arousal switch off" before he reaches a point where his level of self-control makes this too difficult. After a few moments stop interacting with him, be calm and still, and ask him to *sit* or *lie down*.
- If your dog responds, mark and immediately resume playing with him.
- If your dog doesn't respond, step on or hold the leash to prevent him from running off to play somewhere else. Wait for him to offer a *sit* or

down. It shouldn't take long for him to figure out that play will only resume after he remains calm in a *sit* or *down*.

- Gradually increase the length of time you expect him to remain in a *sit* or *down*. Vary the length of these breaks, and include some that are only a few seconds. This way, your dog has many opportunities to succeed and earn the reward of play.

Fetch

The classic game of fetch provides a terrific opportunity for your dog to practice impulse control while having a blast. If your dog already knows how to retrieve an object and release it to you, teach him to wait for your okay before retrieving the object.

- To start, have your dog on leash to prevent him from bolting after the toy.

CHECKLIST

Rules for Tug Games

Contrary to popular advice, tug can be a fun game for canines and humans alike, which also helps your dog learn manners and cooperation. But, like any game, it must be played by the rules.

Rules

Tug is not for every dog. If your dog has guarding issues, games such as fetch are a better choice.

✓ Dogs should only be allowed to play this game with adults.

✓ Your dog must reliably respond to *leave it* with the chosen toy before playing tug with it. Refusing to *leave it* on request ends the game.

✓ Your dog should have access to tug toys only when you are present.

✓ Start with a long tug toy, approximately 3 feet (0.9 meter) in length with a knot in the middle.

✓ If your dog grabs the toy on your side of the knot, the game is over.

✓ Never allow your dog to play "*keep away*" with toys. If your dog plays "keep away," keep him on a leash, keep the toy on a long line, or use two identical toys to rotate between the two and keep your dog focused on playing with you.

✓ Whether it is intentional or accidental, if your dog's teeth touch your skin, this ends the game.

✓ Like all games, tug should be contingent on your dog's good behavior. Ask him to do something before engaging in the game.

✓ Interrupt the game frequently so your dog doesn't become so excited that he loses control.

✓ Barking and growling may or may not indicate aggression during play. Get to know your dog in order to make this judgment.

✓ Cease the play until your dog offers you another *sit*. He will learn that the settling down to wait for the release is the fastest way to earn the reward. For many dogs this is a challenge, because they become excessively excited in this situation.

- Toss the toy a few feet away.
- If he stays seated, mark and give a release word for him to retrieve the toy.
- If he jumps up for the toy before he is released, step forward and onto the toy as you gently use the leash to prevent him from grabbing it. Pick the toy up and drop it again a bit farther away, but from a lower height so it is less enticing for your dog.
- When your dog can wait for a couple of seconds, gradually extend the time before he is released to retrieve the toy.
- Gradually toss the toy farther away, and practice in various environments.

Behavior Problems

ogs inspire us to head outdoors for exercise and to make new friends. They love us unconditionally and provide invaluable comfort and joy. Many studies have confirmed that dogs can improve our lives and health by lowering our anxiety and stress. But, dealing with canine behavior issues can have the opposite effect. Blood pressure rises when you come home to find an unpleasant note from a neighbor complaining of constant barking; when your dog bounces around wildly to greet guests and steals the food you have carefully prepared for them; or when he decides to add a few digging pits to your backyard landscaping.

Why Do Behavior Issues Develop?

A canine activity becomes labeled as a behavior problem when it is exhibited within a context, or to a degree that conflicts with human expectations. For instance:

- Your dog enjoys digging in the yard, but you enjoy the sight of a perfectly manicured lawn.
- Your dog demonstrates his delight when you arrive home in a typical canine manner by racing around, jumping, and barking and howling with delight. But you look forward to a peaceful sanctuary after a hard day at work.
- Your dog uses his spare time pursuing the traditional canine activity of searching his environment for tasty morsels and interesting playthings. You want to use your spare time eating dinner and watching TV, but you discover that he has pulled your dinner off the counter and used the remote control as a chew toy.

Many behavior issues are rationalized as the inevitable consequences of living with a specific breed or type of dog. This is based on the assumption that particular breeds are guaranteed to behave in a certain manner. Of course, some generalizations are true. Sporting dogs are typically energetic, and many terriers love to dig. However, canine behavior is variable and flexible, and this was true long before purebreds existed.

The likelihood and degree to which a dog exhibits certain behaviors is due to genetics, quality of early socialization, prior learning experiences, age, health, and environment. The crucial factor in any dog's environment is his family's ability to address his specific needs. If his needs are not met, behavior issues due to boredom and frustration are more likely. Behavior can also be affected by stress, and dogs vary in their coping ability. For some dogs, moving to a new home is a major source of stress. For others, rearranging the living room furniture can be equally stressful.

TRAINER'S TIP

Owners, especially new puppy parents, are often surprised when behavior problems arise. But, behavior is constantly changing, and it is unrealistic to expect any dog to behave consistently throughout his life without guidance to keep it in the right direction. It is an owner's responsibility to notice these changes and interrupt unwanted behavior before it turns into a habit.

Young dogs sometimes outgrow undesirable behaviors, but it is a mistake to simply wait for a spontaneous recovery. More often, the behavior is likely to become a deeply rooted habit unless you take steps to resolve the problem at an early stage.

Steps to Addressing Behavior Problems

Health Check

Before proceeding with behavior modification, check with your veterinarian to rule out any underlying health or nutritional issues. Especially for senior dogs, a change in behavior may signal a health problem. For example, the pain of arthritis may lower a dog's tolerance for handling and may lead to general crankiness and aggression.

Management to Prevent Practice

Managing your dog and his environment is essential to revising bad habits. It decreases his opportunities to carry out the behavior. It also removes him from triggers that normally encourage it. Fewer opportunities to engage in the behavior will prevent the habit from becoming more ingrained. Practice makes perfect. You do not want to provide more opportunities for your dog to practice an unwanted behavior.

Identify Underlying Causes

For some dogs, very specific triggers will motivate certain behaviors. But in most cases, multiple stimuli trigger the behavior. Consider the factors that motivate your dog's unwanted behavior. Is he stressed, overly aroused, bored, or unsure of what is expected of him? Where was he when the behavior occurred? Who was near him? What was he doing?

Answering these questions will help you identify the specific triggers for a behavior. This makes it possible to plan controlled practice sessions that will encourage him to develop a better response.

Employ Desensitization, Habituation, and Counterconditioning

When you have identified the factors that adversely affect your dog's behavior, you can begin to resolve these issues through desensitization, habituation, and counterconditioning.

Sign Your Dog Up for the "Learn to Earn" Program

In order to revise your dog's behavior, you must limit his access to valued resources, such as food, toys, and attention. Most importantly, you must

TRAINING TRUTH

How Long Does It Take to Resolve Behavior Issues?

In the twenty-first century, many people expect quick results. Unfortunately, there are few quick fixes or shortcuts to resolving behavior issues. Dogs are not computers, and they cannot be reprogrammed with the push of a button. Downloading new information into your dog's behavioral database to override older data requires time and patience. Further, attempting to completely eliminate a normal canine behavior is not a realistic goal. No amount of training can stop behaviors that have been hardwired into the canine psyche for thousands of years.

A better approach is to manage your dog's behavior and gradually refocus his energy and inclinations toward positive outlets. For example, thank him for alerting you with a few barks when someone comes to the door. Then reward him for settling quietly on request. Rather than forbidding him to dig anywhere, provide a special sandbox for this purpose.

The speed and degree to which a behavior can be modified depends greatly on your dog's predisposition for that activity, and the longevity of the habit he has developed. Unfortunately, many pet parents may not notice a developing problem until the behavior is deeply ingrained. They may not take steps to revise it until they fear serious consequences. Furthermore, owners often unwittingly reinforce bad habits by inadvertently rewarding them. If you aren't consistently preventing unwanted behaviors and reinforcing appropriate ones, your inaction is sufficient to reinforce budding bad habits.

Training will eventually improve every dog's behavior, but the degree of improvement and rate of success is contingent on the dog's disposition, age, and prior experiences, as well as the family's training skills. Some training situations are also more challenging. However, they serve to teach us more about our dogs and improve our human-canine teamwork.

revise the way he gains access to those things. In the "Learn to Earn" program, access to resources becomes contingent on mannerly behavior. Your expectations about his behavior should be adjusted according to your dog's age, personality, and level of training. For instance, a dog that already has a working relationship with his family will be more receptive to a behavior modification program.

View Your Dog's Behavior as a Whole: The Circle of Behavior

Each part of your dog's behavior affects every other. Rather than focusing solely on one particular aspect of your dog's behavior that may need improvement, evaluate his overall behavior. For example, if your dog is permitted to jump wildly when greeting guests in your home, don't be surprised if he exhibits a lack of self-control in other situations, such as when walking on leash. Establishing a pattern of mannerly behavior in his daily routine will help him develop better behaviors when he is faced with challenging situations.

Improve Impulse Control

Lack of impulse control can manifest itself in a broad spectrum of behavior problems. A dog without adequate self-control is less able to modify his behavior. This often leads to unacceptable responses to people, places, and things. For example, a dog that lacks impulse control may rush through a doorway, drag his owner down the street, grab food off the counter, or bark excessively to demand attention.

Dogs that are encouraged to develop self-control are more aware of their behavior and are much more receptive to guidance toward appropriate behaviors (see Chapter Eight starting on page 153).

Teach Incompatible Behaviors

If you consistently reward your dog's good behavior, it will occur more frequently. This will also lessen his opportunities and inclination to indulge in bad habits. Better yet, teach your dog to perform a behavior that is incompatible with the unwanted behavior. For example, if he barks at other dogs passing on the street, teach him to look at you whenever dogs pass by.

Avoid Accidentally Reinforcing Unwanted Behaviors

Your behavior has a big impact on your dog's behavior. For example, if your dog is overexcited, barking, and lunging, your normal reaction may be to yell and yank on his leash. Rather than calming him, your behavior intensifies his response to the situation.

Be attentive to your behavior in order to avoid unintentionally reinforcing unwanted habits. For instance, touching or speaking to an excited dog, even saying "*Off*" or "*No jump*" can have the opposite effect. The dog not only becomes more excited; he may find this attention rewarding, despite that fact that it was not positive attention.

Expect Subtle Behavior Changes

Expect gradual improvements when working to correct your dog's behavior issues. Like a car, if an unwanted behavior has been allowed to pick up speed, it will take longer to slow it down. Expecting a longstanding behavior to suddenly cease is unrealistic. The goal is gradual modification, like the slow, comfortable deceleration of a car.

Be Prepared for Frustration Bursts

Modifying an unwanted habit requires patience and persistence. Suppose your dog is in the habit of expecting your immediate attention when he barks. To break this habit, you begin to ignore his barking, and your usual response is not forthcoming. He will most likely become frustrated and try harder to elicit the desired response from you, because this

PAWS TO CONSIDER

Infrequent, occasional rewards can be sufficient to reinforce an ingrained unwanteds habit. Your dog perfected this behavior because, at some point, it was rewarding. This can be compared to a gambler who loves to play slot machines. Even though he loses most of the time and the typical payoff is minimal, he will continue to play the machine, hoping to hit the jackpot. This is called variable ratio of reinforcement. The unpredictable nature of the reward actually *strengthens* the persistence of the behavior.

approach has worked so often in the past. At first, his barking problem will escalate. But, like a gambler who no longer pulls the same lever at an unlucky slot machine, your dog will eventually learn that this behavior no longer works.

Bet on Boredom Busters

Many pet dogs live in a relatively bland, monotonous environment. This lack of mental and physical stimulation can lead to behavior issues. Although it is important to ensure that your dog has adequate physical exercise, attempting to physically exhaust him will only work as a temporary fix for behavior problems. With all this exercise, your dog will develop more stamina, and it will require increasingly more intense workouts to dissipate his energy.

A daily routine that provides a combination of aerobic (physical) and nonaerobic (mental) exercise is vital to any behavior modification program. Enrich your dog's life with appropriate food-stuffed toys, training games, play, and special activities.

It's a Setup!

Just like a sports coach, you should schedule loads of practice sessions prior to the real game. Plan these practice sessions for times when you can be calm and focused, and have time to set up controlled situations that can be designed to gradually simulate real-life scenarios. For example, suppose you are teaching your dog to lie calmly on a mat while you eat dinner. Start by teaching him to go to the mat and remain there, without the distraction of food on the table. When he can do that reliably, begin to work on keeping him on his mat during a real meal.

Consider the Cost of Correction

Punishment may interrupt a behavior in the short term, but it often causes it to escalate later on. It can also lead to unwanted side effects in response to negative associations. Some dogs become anxious, withdrawn, or depressed. They may also become fearful of the punisher or other stimuli in the environment at the time of the punishment. They may resort to biting due to fear and stress. Punishment may raise the dog's arousal level to the point where he responds with retaliatory aggression. Attempting to quell aggression with threatening or pain-inducing techniques such as yelling, poking, pinching, hitting, hissing, rolling, or shocking will more than likely fan the flames and increase the intensity and frequency of aggression.

Some dogs may temporarily shut down, a reaction that is sometimes referred to as learned helplessness. Unfortunately, it encourages the punisher to assume the behavior has been eliminated. In reality, this dog has become a ticking time bomb. He has learned to suppress the typical warning signs of pending aggression. Instead, he may eventually bite without warning.

Constant fear and stress also makes it difficult to be receptive to following your instructions. In contrast, positive training encourages the dog to feel good about the training experience. This translates into a generalized attitude of feeling positive about things associated with training, such as environments, people, or things.

Punishment may also lead the dog to develop owner-absent behaviors. For instance, the dog simply learns to wait for times when the owner is absent before indulging in forbidden activities. Unless you identify the cause of an unwanted behavior and provide an appropriate alternative, it will surely continue in your absence.

BETTER BEHAVIOR

If your dog suffers from any type of fear issues, keep a treat pouch within easy reach so you can work on behavior modification whenever the need arises.

Common Behavior Problems

Barking

Dogs use their voices to communicate many things, and they bark for many good reasons, such as warning us of intruders. However, barking is also one of the most common causes of frustration, concern, and inhumane retribution from pet owners. Excessive barking is a major reason why dogs are surrendered to shelters. Many dogs bark themselves right out of a home.

You must first identify the underlying cause of excessive barking in order to effectively minimize the problem. The intensity, volume, and frequency of barking, as well as your dog's body language and the situation will help you determine the possible underlying cause.

The Alarm Barker

A dog that barks at the presence of intruders can be a valuable asset. In fact, most people want their dogs to let them know when someone has stepped onto their property. It only becomes a problem if your dog does not settle after a few warning barks. Invite friends over to help you practice.

- Have your visitor knock on the door, which will prompt your dog to bark.
- Say "*Thank you*" or "*Good dog*" as you wiggle a high-value treat in front of his nose (which will cause barking to cease). Your dog may be surprised for a moment if he is accustomed to being scolded rather than rewarded for barking. Give him the treat to reward him for being quiet.
- Repeat, repeat, repeat.
- Eventually, your dog will learn to bark briefly when someone knocks, and then look to you in order to be rewarded for a job well done. This approach is also helpful if your dog barks when visitors come in. This will help him develop a positive association with them.

Arrival/Excitement Barking

A dog that barks when entering a new environment is probably expressing over-the-top enthusiasm combined with a lack of impulse control.

When you enter an environment that prompts your dog to bark, simply turn and walk away. When he is quiet, reward him with food and praise, and approach again. This way, he will learn that being quiet allows him to experience new environments. Reinforce this training with the impulse control exercises outlined in Chapter Eight.

The Attention-Seeking Barker

Dogs quickly learn which behaviors are rewarding and which behaviors are not. If your dog is in the habit of barking to demand attention, he has previously discovered that this behavior gets results. This may be personal attention, getting out to play, or convincing you to open the cupboard and give him a biscuit.

When your dog barks for attention, any response from you will be viewed as rewarding. It doesn't matter if you nicely ask him to stop, or yell angrily at the top of your lungs. To revise this behavior, you must teach him that barking for attention will have the opposite effect.

Follow these steps:
- Pretend to read or turn on the TV or computer.
- When he barks, ignore him and turn away.
- When he remains quiet for a moment, turn toward him but don't interact yet.
- When he settles down for about five seconds, approach and praise, then pet and offer him a piece of kibble or a small treat.
- Practice this in other areas of the home as well.

Repeat this exercise until your dog gets the idea that barking causes you to ignore him, but being quiet will get your attention. Rewarding your dog for seeking your attention in a quiet manner captures the appropriate behavior.

If your dog barks when he wants to be taken out for a walk, don't wait for his prompting to tell you that he needs to go out. Instead, take him out at regular intervals.

Spooky Barking

If barking is paired with an attempt to retreat, run, or hide, this may be a response to inadequate socialization or habituation. A dog that has not had adequate positive exposure to people, places, and things may find them scary, and barking is meant to

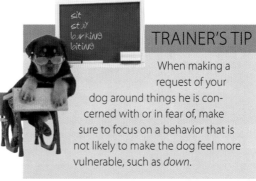

TRAINER'S TIP

When making a request of your dog around things he is concerned with or in fear of, make sure to focus on a behavior that is not likely to make the dog feel more vulnerable, such as *down*.

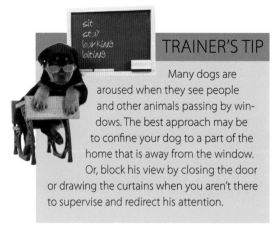

TRAINER'S TIP

Many dogs are aroused when they see people and other animals passing by windows. The best approach may be to confine your dog to a part of the home that is away from the window. Or, block his view by closing the door or drawing the curtains when you aren't there to supervise and redirect his attention.

keep these frightening things at a distance. If this type of situation is not addressed in its early stages, it may evolve into lunging and snapping.

Reprimanding a dog at a time like this is comparable to yelling at a person who is frightened. This will surely create greater stress and worsen the situation.

A better approach is to gradually increase the dog's familiarity and comfort with a wider range of experiences, particularly those that have previously triggered his barking. This process can be accelerated by gradually exposing him to the stimuli from a distance he can tolerate while offering him high-value treats, toys, and other rewards. The goal is to help him develop a positive association between the thing he fears and things he loves. If you received one hundred dollars every time an intimidating person entered your room, you would learn to happily anticipate this person's arrival.

Steps to Resolve Spooky Barking:

- Identify what is triggering the barking. Consider the context as well. For instance, your dog may bark at men with beards when they enter your home, but not when he sees them on the street.
- Identify your dog's threshold (the distance at which the barking is triggered). If it is 50 feet (15.2 meters), then start introducing him to the source of his fear at a distance of at least 60 feet (18.3 meters), so you are working sub-threshold.
- Offer high-value rewards from your hand, or toss them on the ground every time he is exposed to the thing he fears.
- When your dog develops the habit of looking to you for a treat every time he sees the trigger, you can begin asking him to do something like sitting or hand targeting to get the treat. This gives him an alternative positive behavioral response to something that was once a negative trigger.
- Gradually decrease the distance between your dog and the trigger. If at any point he ceases to respond reliably to your requests, backtrack and practice in a less challenging manner.

If your dog barks because he is fearful of a specific adult family member, arrange for that person to take a more active role in the dog's care, such as feeding, walking, and training. This way, your dog learns that many rewarding things come from this family member.

Yard and Barrier Barking

The backyard can be an enjoyable place for your dog, but if he is left alone he may get bored. As a result, he may alleviate boredom by patrolling the area and barking to alert to any possible human or animal intruders. From the dog's perspective, he is simply doing his job to protect the property. This behavior is reinforced by the adrenaline rush that results from successfully driving away any real or imagined intruder. Leaving your dog alone in the yard may also encourage him to indulge in other inappropriate activities, such as digging or escaping. More importantly, he is vulnerable to dangers, such as being stolen, poisoned, or hurt by an animal that enters the yard.

Dogs are usually relegated to the yard because they don't behave well in the house. Giving your dog a few stuffed chew toys and confining him to a pet-safe area is a more effective way to prevent barking and other unwanted habits.

During supervised playtime in the yard, keep your dog on leash at first. This will give you a gentle and effective means of preventing him from charging at the fence and barking. Watch for initial cues that he is focusing on something that might prompt him to bark. Be proactive by redirecting him before it happens. It may help to work on this issue before his normal mealtime, or reward him with a toy that he has not been allowed to play with for a few days.

Separation Issues

Dogs are highly social creatures and prefer to be in the company of their family. But, it is a fact of life that all dogs will be left alone at times. For some dogs this can result in boredom, anxiety, and extreme distress. As a result, they may

DANGER!

If you suspect that your dog suffers from the most severe form of separation distress—separation anxiety—he should first be evaluated by your veterinarian. A behavior professional should work with you to design a systematic program to gradually acclimate your dog to the idea of spending time alone. During this behavior modification program, alternatives to leaving your dog alone should be employed, such as dog walkers, sitters, or daycare. Although this problem is painful for all involved, when approached methodically it can usually be resolved.

engage in behaviors like excessive barking, destructive chewing, house soiling, and attempts to escape. If your dog is exhibiting separation issues, he may be bored because of insufficient mental or physical exercise, or he may not have been adequately prepared to spend time alone.

Avoid "Velcro Dog Syndrome" by Practicing Semi-Absences

Showering your dog with attention when you are home may alleviate your guilt about leaving him alone at other times. However, this approach can cause him to become accustomed to constant companionship. As a result, any eventual separation becomes more traumatic when you must leave. Get him used to this idea by encouraging him to enjoy quiet moments by himself while you are home. Teach him to self-pacify with chew toys, which will ultimately soften the blow of your departure. When you have a day off, make sure your dog still spends short periods of time away from you throughout the day.

Training Your Dog to Spend Time Alone:

- Prevent your dog from constantly following you around the house by using leash tethering, a crate, a gated area, or an exercise pen. Arrange for your dog to spend ten to twenty minutes

BREAKING THE HABIT

Jumping Up

Jumping is an attention-seeking behavior—an outlet for energy and adrenaline—and it indicates a lack of impulse control. It is also self-reinforcing. The act of jumping and making physical contact with you is rewarding to your dog. For this reason, prevention is the key to breaking the habit. Ignore him when he jumps, and teach him an alternative behavior that is incompatible (something your dog cannot do while jumping), such as standing or sitting. Your dog will soon realize that jumping earns no reward, but not jumping earns a variety of rewards, such as praise and attention. Dogs can quickly learn to exert self-control in stimulating situations, such as when greeting people.

Steps to cultivate his self-control and discourage jumping:
- Tether your dog to a stable object when first introducing him to this training concept.
- Walk toward him. If he stands still or *sits*, move forward and follow through by petting him. If he jumps, lunges, or bounces around, stop and turn away or take a few steps back. Be sure to time this feedback to coincide with his actions.
- Once you are close enough to greet your dog, and he has four paws on the floor, mark his action with a *"Yes"* or the clicker, and reward him with a treat and calm praise.
- Be prepared to halt all interactions with your dog as soon as his paws come off the floor.
- Practice this anti-jumping exercise in every possible scenario: in different rooms, when your dog is behind a gate or in his crate, when you are preparing his meals, or when you are opening the door.
- Help him to generalize the concept of a polite greeting by enlisting family and visitors to practice with him.
- This technique can be modified when you are taking walks and your dog greets people who have not been instructed on how to respond to his unwanted jumping. Step on his leash when he greets people until he reliably keeps four paws on the floor. This way, your dog can say hello without having the opportunity to reinforce his jumping.

at a time resting in this area with chew toys while you read a book or watch TV.
- At first, remain nearby. When he becomes able to focus on a chew toy, gradually increase the distance, and eventually remain in another room during these practice sessions.
- Slowly increase the time he is alone from five to ten to fifteen minutes (and so on). Vary the length of your absence and the location where he is left alone. This will help him generalize this skill. It also helps your dog understand that your departure doesn't necessarily indicate a prolonged absence.
- Eventually, your dog will be comfortable being left alone for longer periods of time, whether you are home or not.

- Make your entrances and departures low-key and minimize clues that usually alert him of your departure, such as picking up your keys and putting on your coat. Instead, offer your dog treats and toys before you leave so that these triggers become associated with positive experiences rather than predicting your departure.

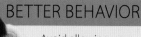

BETTER BEHAVIOR

Avoid allowing your dog to greet visitors at your front door until he has developed impulse control in practice sessions. This prevents him from rushing to a door to say hello. Dogs tend to behave far better when they are brought in to meet visitors after they have settled.

Digging

Digging is a normal part of a dog's behavioral agenda. Dogs dig to keep cool, to bury valuables, to hunt for vermin, and to have fun. Some dogs are so devoted to digging that they can transform a yard into the equivalent of an archeological site. If your dog has a strong desire to dig, it is easier and more fair to focus on redirecting his behavior to an appropriate outlet rather than attempting to extinguish it altogether.

The following are management techniques to control unwanted digging:
- Teach your dog to respond to his name and come away from an intended digging spot when called.
- Allow him to spend time in the yard only when supervised by an adult to prevent unauthorized digging.
- If possible, provide a digging pit—an area with soft soil or sand. Bury some of his toys and give him permission to excavate. Keep this area securely covered when not in use; otherwise, neighborhood animals might choose this as their potty spot.

Chasing Behaviors

Certain dogs are specifically bred to have a strong instinct to chase, such as sighthounds and herding dogs. In these cases, chasing is used for a purpose that suits our needs. However, chasing cats, children, skateboarders, or cars is dangerous for all, including the dog. It is also easily reinforced because the dog often successfully drives the car, person, or other animal away.

The solution to this problem is careful management to prevent chasing; training to ensure that your dog reliably comes back when called; and providing an outlet for him to chase appropriate items, such as a ball or Frisbee, in a safe location like a fenced yard.

Do not allow your dog off leash until he has a good foundation in basic manners and you are certain that he will come back when called. Also work on improving his impulse control. Practice with your dog on leash when he is around things he previously chased; do this at a controlled distance with high-value rewards.

Boldly Begging

Some dogs master the art of an intense stare, while others focus on nudging, poking, and pawing. However, when these behaviors happen at mealtimes, all have the same goal in mind: convincing us to share our food. Begging at the table can range from mildly annoying to outright invasive.

Rather than becoming frustrated, envision the behavior you would like from your dog at mealtime, and train him to do just that. In the meantime, management is the first step to resolving a begging problem. This can be accomplished by tethering him to a stable object away from the table where he can rest on a mat with a chew toy. Or, you can put him in his crate or confine him to another room to prevent him from begging at the table.

If you would like to teach your dog to rest a distance away from you during mealtimes, consult page 136, which focuses on teaching your dog to target to a mat.

Do not work on this training while you are preparing or eating a meal. Schedule practice sessions for other times of the day.

Eating Stool: Coprophagia

Many dogs indulge in eating stool—their own or that of other animals. Mother dogs eat their pups' stool to keep the whelping area clean, and pups may mimic this behavior, especially when left in a confined area with their own feces. Some dogs indulge due to boredom or stress; some do it to tidy up or because they consider it a delicacy. It may also be due to an underlying medical cause, such as lack of sufficient nutrients in the diet, so be sure to check with your veterinarian to rule this out.

If your dog is eating his own waste, the problem is fairly easy to resolve. Promptly discard of feces so your dog does not have access to it. When possible, remove your dog from the area prior to cleanup to prevent accidentally increasing the perceived value of feces.

If your dog is indulging in cat litter box raids, put the box in an area where your dog can't have access to it, or confine him to an area away from the box.

Avoid reprimanding your dog for this behavior. He may simply wait to do so when you are gone. If you catch your dog in the act, remain calm, as your urgency might exacerbate the problem.

Inappropriate Chewing: Dog of Mass Destruction

Puppies chew to alleviate teething pain, and this activity continues into adulthood for several reasons. Dogs chew to alleviate boredom, to investigate, and simply because it is enjoyable. Unauthorized chewing is likely to

dramatically increase if a dog is deprived of sufficient mental and physical exercise. The goal is not to prevent your dog from chewing. Instead, teach him to chew appropriate items, because canine-chewing sprees can result in dangerous and expensive consequences.

Careful management and supervision is necessary until the dog has developed a strong, reliable habit of chewing only appropriate objects. This is especially important for young dogs and those who are enthusiastic about investigating the home. The use of supervised tethering, a crate for short-term confinement, and a long-term confinement area such as an exercise pen or pet-safe room should be employed.

Follow these steps to manage a chewing problem:

- Dog-proof your home by keeping potentially dangerous items out of the dog's reach, such as electric cables, cleaning supplies, nylon socks, TV remotes, and

DANGER!

If you come home to find your dog has been destructive, never reprimand him. He cannot make any connection between his past behavior and a current punishment. However, he is likely to make a connection between your arrival home and being punished. This will cause increased stress and destructiveness. It will also undermine your dog's trust in you.

shoes. Remember that enthusiastic chewers may focus their efforts on the floor or wall moldings.

- Invest in a variety of chew toys appropriate for your dog's age, chewing strength, and enthusiasm.
- Food stuffing increases the value of chew toys. Provide some that offer instant gratification by easily dispensing the food. Others should be more challenging.
- Prevent your dog from gaining weight by using some or all of his daily food to stuff his toys. Keep him interested in the toys by rotating them every day.
- If your dog chews something inappropriate, redirect him to "legal" toys.

Grand Theft Canine

We have put the canine drive to investigate and hunt for us to good use. Unfortunately, it can also prompt dogs to hunt around the house, and their "prey" becomes our shoes, remote controls, and dinner waiting to be served on the kitchen counter.

You can decrease the thrill of the inappropriate hunt by employing management techniques and avoiding accidental encouragement, such as chasing your dog to retrieve their loot. You would not leave the keys in your car to tempt a car thief. Likewise, you should not leave valuables around your home if you have a canine kleptomaniac. That means clearing counters, locking trash bins, and putting children's toys out of reach.

If your dog does get something he should not have, resist the urge to chase him around to recover it. This is a prime example of unwittingly rewarding a dog for unwanted behavior. Most dogs love to play the "chase" game, as well as the "keep away" game with items of perceived value.

Instead, implement better management. If your dog is trailing a leash, you will be able to stop him in his tracks by stepping on it or taking hold of the end. Then ask him to drop the item (see object exchange exercise on page 191). If he is not wearing his leash, kneel and pretend to investigate something on the ground. This should encourage him to come close to investigate what you have found, and you can then retrieve the item. Also, work on improving his response to coming when called.

Resource Guarding

Resource guarding is the most common behavior associated with aggression. Defending resources such as food, bones, toys, sleeping locations, and favored people is a normal, adaptive canine trait. However, in a human environment it can be extremely dangerous. Dogs must learn that there is no need to guard their resources from people.

Resource guarding directed at people is a serious behavior issue that should be addressed immediately. In many cases, resource guarding

directed at other dogs is best dealt with through management. Manage the environment by supervising, or separate the dogs to prevent them from feeling stressed or aroused when playing with toys or eating their food.

Some of the warning signs of resource guarding are obvious, such as growling and snapping. However, others are more subtle, such as carrying food and toys to secluded locations; covering them with his paw or body; and becoming stiff or tense, or gulping his food when people or other dogs approach. Some dogs only guard certain things they consider especially valuable or important. They may also do this when they feel less secure. For example, your dog may become more protective toward his toys when another dog visits your home.

Your immediate reaction might be to scold your dog. Positive training is a preferable course of action. Teach him to feel comfortable when someone approaches his perceived valuables, and to relinquish them when you ask. This requires a gradual approach. If he displays a guarding reaction during these training sessions, you have progressed too quickly.

During this training, don't let your dog have access to anything that might trigger aggression outside these controlled practice sessions. If your dog gets a hold of something that he is apt to guard, avoid a stand-off. Toss him an especially enticing toy or treat. He will probably drop the contraband item, and you can safely take it.

Training to Discourage Resource Guarding

These exercises should be done in a location where your dog has not previously shown aggression. Practice at a pace that allows your dog to feel comfortable each step of the way, so he feels no need to resort to aggression. Additionally, safety is of utmost concern. Therefore, keep your dog on leash and tethered to a stable object, and stay out of his reach in case he does become aggressive.

If you are trying to discourage his habit of food guarding, begin by hand-feeding him. This helps him understand that food comes from people. Once that is established, you can move on to exercises that address the specifics of what your dog has a propensity to guard.

Food Bowl Guarding

- Place the food on a plate or in a low-rimmed bowl. It's easier to evaluate your dog's facial gestures if he cannot bury his face in the bowl.
- Place one piece of food in the dish. While holding the dish, let your dog eat the food.
- Take it away and offer him a more delectable treat from your hand.
- Repeat this exercise until your dog seems comfortable.
- The next step is to put several pieces of food in the bowl, allow him to eat a few, and remove the bowl before he has finished. Reward him by offering a better treat from your other hand.
- Slowly work toward holding the dish closer to the floor.

- Next, place a dish containing food on the floor and keep your hand on it. This is a time to be extra cautious. When your dog lifts his head out of the bowl for a treat, toss a bit of food away from the bowl and remove the bowl.
- If you notice any signs of tension or aggression, you have progressed too quickly. Your dog should be comfortable and cooperative when you remove the bowl rather than grudgingly tolerating it.

Getting Your Dog Accustomed to Food Bowl Approaches

- Place an empty bowl on the floor near your dog.
- Approach, place a few pieces of dry food in it, and step away.
- When the dog finishes eating, approach and toss a few more pieces of food in the bowl.
- When your dog is accustomed to this step of the exercise, approach him while he is eating and toss a bonus treat into his bowl. The goal is to teach him to look forward to you approaching the bowl.
- When he has finished the food in his bowl, pick it up and offer him a tasty treat.
- Eventually, you should be able to take the bowl away when there is still food in it. Take the bowl, add the bonus treat, and return the bowl to the ground.
- If your dog has developed a habit of guarding his food bowl, you should periodically refresh his training by tossing high-value treats into his bowl.

Object Exchange Game

Try this game to correct your dog's habit of guarding objects such as toys and chew bones. The basic principle of the game is to take something away from your dog, offer something better in exchange, and then give back the first item. This will teach him to look forward to having things taken away.

- Start with items your dog is less interested in (such as a dry biscuit or a less preferred toy), and gradually work up to higher ticket items.

- Hold the item in your hand and allow your dog to check it out while you hold it. Let him take the item.
- Give him a treat to encourage him to relinquish it and then give the item right back.
- Repeat, repeat, repeat.
- Give the item to your dog for a count of three, then take it away and immediately offer your dog a high-value food reward. Then give the item back.

- Repeat, repeat, repeat.
- As your dog improves, allow him to keep the item for longer periods before taking it.
- Gradually work with slightly higher value items as you practice this exercise.
- If he displays any signs of aggression, you have progressed too quickly or added too many challenges to the exercise at this stage in his training.

Rules for Children

Dogs can enhance your child's self-esteem, sense of responsibility, and empathy. However, many dogs feel overwhelmed and stressed by the high energy, erratic movements, and in some cases, a child's deliberate or accidental antagonism. It can be challenging to facilitate a positive, fun, and safe relationship between dogs and children. Set them up for success by implementing rules for both, creating a safe zone for your dog to rest undisturbed, and encouraging your children to assist with your dog's feeding, watering, and training.

Some dogs respond aggressively to seemingly benign interactions with children, such as petting, bending over, or speaking to the dog. However, most aggressive incidents result from anxiety and pain-inducing incidents, such as a child grabbing or pushing the dog, being very loud, or encroaching on the dog's food or space.

Dogs that are raised with well-mannered, carefully supervised children are more likely to succeed in this area of human relationships. However, some dogs (especially those with a low threshold for excitability and fear) may never successfully adapt to children. Likewise, some children do not have enough impulse control to safely and successfully interact with dogs.

If you are endeavoring to improve your dog's relationships with children, it is essential to ensure safety through vigilant supervision and management during this training. Encourage your children to adhere to rules that will make your dog's interactions with them non-threatening and positive.

- Never approach a strange dog.
- Don't pet dogs on top of the head; instead, scratch them under the chin.
- Don't disturb a dog while he is eating or sleeping.
- Don't stare at dogs; this can turn into something like a showdown.
- No hard hugging or squeezing, wrestling, poking, or pulling on the dog's fur or body parts.
- Do not pick dogs up.

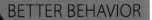

BETTER BEHAVIOR

Allowing your dog to sleep in bed with you does not automatically encourage territorial behavior, nor does it encourage the idea that your dog shares equal status with you. However, your dog may perceive your bed as a valuable resource. If you choose to allow him to sleep in your bed, you should use this privilege as leverage to encourage mannerly behavior. It should only be granted to dogs that willingly move aside when asked. Any dog that growls or snaps rather than moves when asked is not ready for bed privileges. You need to improve his compliance. Begin practicing this first in locations that he considers less valuable. Then practice on the bed with the dog on leash, and finally, practice with the dog off leash.

Aggression

Aggression issues range widely in type, severity, and frequency. It can be directed at people or other animals. Human-directed aggression is certainly of utmost concern. Aggression toward strangers and visitors is usually fear-based and due to a lack of early, adequate socialization. Aggression directed at adult family members is usually motivated by resource guarding or handling issues.

Aggression toward other dogs falls into three general categories: to dogs outside the home when the dog is on leash, to dogs outside the home when the dog is off leash, and to canine housemates.

Treatment of Aggression

When dealing with aggression, it is wise to enlist the aid of a qualified professional. This is not quite the same as teaching new behaviors like sit or down. Treatment of aggression involves changing an emotional response. This requires an accurate understanding of your dog's body language and a serious commitment to management, remedial socialization, desensitization, and counterconditioning. The goal is to help your dog develop a positive association between the stimulus and his aggressive response. Strict adherence to the program will produce gradual progress rather than immediate results.

Ideally, this sort of program maintains progress by working at a level that is always below the dog's threshold level.

TRAINING TRUTH

The Early Warning Signs

Every dog has the potential to bite. The fact that your dog has never done this before does not rule out the possibility. Owners may also fail to recognize the factors that may provoke their dog to bite. These are a few of the reasons why owners neglect to address this type of behavior problem at an early stage.

Most dogs exhibit plenty of warning signs before they actually bite. They use highly ritualized gestures to convey threats and settle disagreements without resorting to actual fighting The warning signals that precede aggression are meant to convey the dog's anxiety. If these indicators go unheeded, the dog may be forced to move on to a more intense aggressive display. From the dog's point of view, biting is the last resort after his repertoire of threats, posturing, and bluffing have failed. Recognizing these subtle warning signs allows you to intervene before your dog begins to experiment with biting, which can lead to serious aggression issues.

A dog's response to threats can include:

- Cringing
- Looking Away
- Avoidance (moving away or attempting to hide)
- Lip Licking
- Yawning
- Excessive Panting
- Becoming tense or immobile
- Ear twitching
- Ears and tail held lower than normal
- Staring
- Growling
- Snarling
- Barking
- Snapping
- Lunging

Aggressive displays can range from a growl to a full-blown attack. Once a dog has behaved aggressively, especially if he has bitten, you should plan on careful management and supervision throughout his lifetime. This can mean keeping your dog muzzled, leashed, or completely separate from children.

Bite Thresholds

Dogs with aggression issues are often labeled as "mean" or "bad." As a result, owners may be reluctant to acknowledge their pet's problem. They may also underestimate the potential risk of dog bites. The severity of a bite can range from touching the skin without leaving any mark to bruising or puncture wounds.

When a dog bites without leaving a mark, it is often assumed that the dog missed. However, dogs have incredibly good eye-mouth coordination. It is more likely that the dog meant this bite as a warning, and injurious biting has not yet become his preferred way to deal with conflict.

Puppies learn to control their bite power at a very young age as they play fight with their dam and littermates. These early experiences play a part in the difference between a dog that bites without causing serious injury and a dog that inflicts serious injury, whenever he feels compelled to defend himself.

Every dog has a different tolerance threshold before he will resort to biting. Subtle or mild aggressive displays may escalate if the dog is confronted by an especially threatening situation. For instance, a dog that is uncomfortable but not aggressive around children may be uncomfortable but tolerant in the presence of one child. If he is forced to cope with attention from several children, he may feel overwhelmed and resort to aggression.

Dog-to-Dog Aggression

Even the most benign dog scuffle can look and sound alarming. In fact, much of friendly, non-threatening ritualized play behavior, such as mouthing, chasing, and mounting can seem to straddle a fine line between fun and fight.

Early, ongoing socialization helps a dog develop the requisite familiarity with dog language and manners in order to have safe interactions. However, even well-socialized dogs may develop aggression issues toward other dogs. Sometimes this is specific and directed at particular dogs or types of dogs. It can also surface as more generalized aggression. In some cases, dog-to-dog aggression is so severe and potentially dangerous that play with other dogs may need to be eliminated.

On-Leash Aggression

Many pet parents are perplexed when their otherwise mild-mannered, friendly canine becomes a barking, snarling maniac when passing other dogs while on leash. In some cases, the dog becomes excited and pulls toward the other dog to interact. The person at the end of the leash yanks back, tightening the leash and communicating tension. Eventually, the dog may develop a negative association about passing dogs on leash. A tightened leash may also trigger the opposition reflex, causing the dog to lean forward. Other dogs may perceive this posture as threatening. Leash tension interferes with natural body language and communication meant to indicate non-threatening intent.

Even if his intent is friendly, it's not a good idea to allow your dog to lunge at other dogs. This habit discourages him from walking politely and paying attention to you. It is also inconsiderate. Some dogs are not interested in greeting other dogs on the street. If forced to do so, they may go into fight mode since the leash prevents them from avoiding the encounter. Social encounters on the street should be limited. Instead, when appropriate, your dog should have plenty of opportunities to socialize in a safe, enclosed environment where he can offer uninhibited calming signals and retreat when necessary.

On-leash greetings generally don't fall into the category of valuable social experiences. Your dog should learn to pass by other dogs without incident. A front-clip harness or head halter makes it easier to guide him away from potentially volatile situations, and prevent him from straining forward.

- Be sure to bring high-value treats along on walks, and walk your dog when he is hungry. This makes it easy to reward him when he passes by another dog without incident. Hand-feed your dog and/or toss treats on the ground away from the other dog and encourage him to find them. This will encourage him to focus on hunting for the food, which sends non-threatening signals to the other dog (e.g., sniffing your hand or the ground).
- Arrange for your dog to pass calm, well-behaved dogs in an environment that allows you to keep him at a distance. This will ensure that he does not become overly aroused. Also, direct your dog in an arc rather than a straight line when passing, which is less threatening for both dogs. Keep moving at a moderate pace. Stopping can increase your dog's anxiety, and moving too quickly may arouse the other dog.
- Play the training game with your dog by asking him to do things he knows well, such as hand targeting. This acts as a distraction and confidence booster. It is also an effective means of classical conditioning, because your dog receives high-value rewards when he is on leash around other dogs.
- If your dog begins to show any signs of aggression toward another dog during these exercises, move away but do not give him a verbal or physical reprimand. Take steps to better control his environment, such as scheduling his walks at times and on routes when you are less likely to encounter other dogs.
- Vary the customary route of your walk so he becomes accustomed to different dogs and begins to generalize this concept.
- When he is ready, walk him with calm, well-socialized dogs.

- If he likes stuffed toys, encourage him to carry one when he passes other dogs. This serves as a reward and prevents him from barking.

Dog-to-Dog Aggression in the Home

Many people successfully share their lives with two or more dogs. However, the dynamic in a multi-dog household can vary greatly depending on the mix of dogs and the behavior of human family members. It isn't unusual for dogs to become possessive toward toys and other valued items in the presence of other dogs—even housemates. However, dogs in the same household most often become possessive toward a favorite person.

Do some detective work to assess the scope of the problem. Have there been injuries? Is there a distinct size or strength difference between the dogs? Do the dogs tend to fight when people are absent or present?

Don't jump to conclusions about which dog is initiating fights. Explosive displays of growling, lunging, and snarling are usually the culmination of many unfriendly encounters. Outright aggression is preceded by subtle behaviors that owners may fail to notice unless they are paying close attention.

If your dogs begin showing signs of confrontational behavior toward one another, intervene before it escalates into an actual fight. Do not punish either dog or encourage one or the other to be more assertive. The most effective intervention is managing their daily routine by controlling their access to the environment, sleeping areas, toys, food, and people. Condition them to be more comfortable and calm around each other. This can feel like a daily juggling act, but is an absolute necessity.

If the situation has progressed to actual fighting, or you suspect that it is imminent, keep the dogs safely separated at all times when they are unsupervised. Continue this safety measure throughout the retraining process.

Begin working on measures that will encourage the dogs to remain calm and peaceful together.

- Each dog should have enough personal space during mealtime to discourage them from behaving protectively with their food. You may need to keep them completely separate or crated to prevent mealtime altercations.
- Each dog should have ample toys to keep them occupied, but they should have access to these only when they are separated for the same reasons as above.
- Each should have a safe, comfortable, private resting spot. This will discourage them from competing for coveted sleeping areas.
- Each dog should receive adequate attention from you.
- Each dog should have opportunities to play the training game with you separately and together.

Dog Park Fights

Dog parks are a mixed blessing. They provide valuable opportunities for dogs to play off leash in a safely confined area. However, the mixture of dogs in a public park changes from moment to moment. This in turn changes the social dynamic, stress level, and the potential for squabbles. The success and safety of a dog park experience is contingent on several factors. Most importantly, owners must be realistic about their dog's suitability for this environment. This may not be a good choice for dogs that have a history of squabbling, causing injuries, or guarding objects they may find at a park (including sticks) that you can't control. Alternative off-leash play may be more appropriate for dogs like this.

You can ensure a harmonious and safe dog park experience by following these steps:

- Recognize the signs of escalating tension, and manage your dog accordingly. For example, if your dog becomes rowdy during play and is not yet skilled at modifying his behavior, his playmates must be chosen carefully.
- Prevent your dog from bullying. Observe his behavior and interrupt him when necessary. This is unfair to the other dogs in the park, and another dog will inevitably retaliate, resulting in a fight.
- Make sure your dog reliably comes when called. This ensures that you can quickly remove him from a situation at the first sign of trouble.
- Pay attention to your dog at all times.
- If you feel that another dog is out of control or posing a threat, leave with your dog.

Physical and Mental Activity

Your dog's mind is a terrible thing to waste. Provide opportunities for him to use his intelligence by partnering with him in fun activities. Most dogs enjoy just about any activity they can share with their family. There are plenty of possibilities to consider, including tricks, games, organized dog sports, and bona fide jobs. Consider your dog's personality, health, and age when choosing appropriate activities for him.

Tricks

Teaching your dog tricks may not have an obvious practical value, but the benefits are far reaching. It will build his confidence and body awareness, improve your communication skills, and teach you to work as a team.

Take a Spin

The cuteness of any trick increases exponentially when you come up with a clever cue. For spin, try something like "*Chase your tail.*"

Shaping Method
1. Wait for your dog to turn his head slightly to one side, then mark and reward.
2. Gradually mark and reward movements that more closely approximate a full turn.
3. When he has learned to make a full circle, add a name to the behavior and say it just before your dog offers the spin.
4. Practice in varying environments.

Targeting Method
1. Teach your dog to touch his nose to the end of a target stick (see page 135).
2. Move the target stick a few inches to one side of your dog so he has to bend his body in a slight curve to follow it. Mark and reward.
3. Gradually move the target stick further around your dog's body to encourage him to turn into a more complete curve. Do this until he is turning in a full circle.

The Benefits of Extracurricular Canine Activities

Don't underestimate the value of recreational activities for your dog. They are much more than simple fun and games. Providing an outlet for his mental and physical energy is one of the best ways to prevent a host of problem behaviors. Every activity and dog sport presents different challenges, but they all offer you opportunities to guide your dog's behavior in a positive direction.

They also provide opportunities for your dog to socialize with both people and dogs, and to practice his social skills.

The challenge of learning new skills can also delay cognitive degeneration, which is especially important for senior dogs.

Recreational activities also ensure that his natural instincts are channeled in acceptable directions. For instance, providing an outlet for your dog's desire to dig can become a fun form of exercise and a way for you and your dog to enjoy the outdoors together. All you need is a pile of leaves or snow, and a few toys and treats on hand to encourage your dog to dig away to find the buried treasure.

Most importantly, both you and your dog will feel better. Exercise and play triggers the release of endorphins ("feel-good" chemicals) in the brain. Both you and your dog will get a kick out of each and every moment spent together having fun.

4. When your dog is making a full circle, add a name to the behavior and say it just prior to moving the target stick.
5. Gradually fade out the use of the target stick by making a briefer movement with it.

Luring Method

1. Hold a food treat at your dog's nose, and move your hand clockwise or counter-clockwise (depending on which direction your dog seems most comfortable turning) to encourage him to turn to one side. Some dogs will easily turn in a full circle, while others may get stuck halfway. If this is the case, mark and reward as he gradually increases his turn to complete a full circle.
2. When your dog is smoothly turning in a circle to follow the treat, try to make the same hand movement without a treat in your hand. Mark and reward him from the other hand.
3. Add a verbal cue just prior to making the hand movement. Continue to mark and reward for every correct spin response.
4. Refine your hand signal, making a slightly narrower circle above your dog's head, and try to stand a little more upright while doing this.

Rollover

This trick will also enhance your dog's trust in you because he must expose his abdomen, and this is a vulnerable position. It can also work as a barometer for your dog's comfort level. After he learns this trick, it is always a good sign when he does it happily.

Luring Method

1. Ask or lure your dog into a *down*.

2. Move a treat to the side of his cheek so he will turn his head slightly and shift his weight to one hip.
3. Move the treat across his shoulder area so he lies flat on his side.

4. Now move your hand over to the floor.
5. For some dogs, gently tickling their abdomen helps. It may also help to teach this trick on a soft surface like a carpet or bed.

6. If your dog does not roll over after a few tries, reward him incrementally so he knows he's on the right track.

Paws Up

For this trick your dog will learn to place his paws on an elevated object like the seat of a chair or a step stool.

1. Place the object in front of your dog and wait for him to move toward it.
2. Mark and reward.
3. Gradually mark and reward for more paw contact with the object.
4. When you are confident the dog is about to do the behavior, add the cue just prior.

Say Your Prayers

In this trick your dog will learn to hold his paws up as if in a prayer position.

1. Ask your dog to sit and use a lure to help him raise his body into a sitting up position.
2. Mark and reward any movement of his paws upward.
3. Gradually reserve a mark and reward for paws up that more closely resemble a prayer position.
4. Add a cue word just prior to his doing so.

Are Your Tired?/Head Down

Teaching your dog to place his head charmingly on the ground or an object, such as a lap, on cue is a great way to jumpstart his career as a photographic model.

Capturing Method

1. Schedule this training session when your dog is a bit tired.
2. Wait for him to *lie down*. Watch closely so you can mark and reward the moment he rests his head on the ground.

3. Repeat.
4. When you are confident that your dog is just about to put his head on the ground, say a cue word before he does it.
5. Gradually increase the duration of the behavior by delaying the mark and reward.

Luring or Targeting

1. Ask your dog to *lie down*.
2. Move the treat lure or the target to the ground just in front of your dog's nose.
3. When he lowers his head to the ground, mark and reward.
4. Repeat.
5. Gradually make your hand movement subtler and add the cue word prior to the hand movement.

Shake

This trick is a tried-and-true favorite. Presenting your hand with palm facing up will be the cue, and a verbal request such as "*Shake*" or "*Hello*" can be added.

Capturing Method

1. Ask your dog to *sit*.
2. Show him a tasty treat and then move your hand a few inches away.
3. Watch your dog's feet, and mark and reward if he begins to move a front paw off the ground.
4. Gradually mark and reward for more movement of his paw off the ground.
5. Present your upturned hand close to your dog's paw just before he lifts it.
6. When he can do this consistently, add the verbal cue.

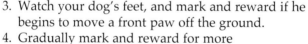

Luring Method

1. Ask your dog to *sit*.
2. Position your hand near the floor near your dog's paw, where it will be ready to catch his paw when it comes off the floor. Do not grab or lift his paw; wait for your dog to lift it himself.
3. Hold a treat in your other hand and position it in front of his nose. Move it slightly to the side, away from the other paw. Your dog will

lean over slightly, which will cause him to lift (very slightly in some cases) the other paw.
4. Mark and reward.

High Five and Wave

For both of these tricks, the cue will be your raised hand with your palm facing your dog. For the high five, position your hand where your dog's paw will be when it is raised. For the wave, move your hand a bit farther away. This trick can be more challenging for short-legged dogs.

Capturing Method
1. Let your dog sniff the treat and hold it in front of him.
2. When he raises his paw to solicit the treat, mark and reward.
3. Repeat.
4. Slowly move your hand higher so your dog will raise his paw higher.
5. When you are confident that he is just about to raise his paw, say the cue word just before he does. Mark and reward.

Sleeping Beauty/Play Possum

This trick is also known as "play dead." You can teach your dog to lie still on his side in response to a variety of creative cues, such as "*Did you drink the witches potion?*" or "*Bang.*" The release word can be equally creative, such as "*You've been kissed by the prince,*" or "*It was a blank bullet!*"

Luring Method
1. Ask or lure your dog to *lie down*.

2. Hold a treat in front of his nose, and move your hand slightly toward his hip that is facing up. This will encourage him to curl to the side.
3. Lower your hand to the floor so his head follows and he is lying flat. Mark and reward.
4. Repeat and add a cue just prior to making your hand movement.
5. Gradually delay the mark and reward after your dog is lying flat, so he will play possum longer.

Are You Bashful?

Few things are cuter than a dog covering his muzzle with his paw in response to a cue like *"Are you bashful?"*

1. Gently touch the side of his muzzle. This will likely prompt him to wipe his face with his paw.
2. Mark and reward when he does.
3. Repeat.
4. Lessen the muzzle touch and wait for him to offer the behavior of wiping his face with his paw. Mark and reward.
5. Add the verbal cue right before he is about to offer the behavior.

Sit Pretty

Luring Method

Very large or long-backed dogs may find this trick challenging.

1. Ask your dog to *sit* so that his rear is close to a couch, chair, or wall. This will help to support him when he sits on his hind legs.
2. Hold a treat close to his nose and slowly lift it up. Mark and reward when one or both of his paws come off the floor even slightly while his rear stays on the floor. Be careful not to reward him for lifting his rear to jump for the treat.
3. Gradually encourage him to consistently lift both front paws off the floor.
4. When he is consistently able to *sit* with his rear on the floor and both paws lifted up, delay the mark and reward for a couple of seconds.
5. Your dog will need to improve his balance and build up muscle strength to support himself in this position.
6. Add the cue just prior to making the hand movement for the dog to sit up.

Bow

Teaching your dog to *bow* on cue is an adorable ending to a routine of tricks. Because it involves stretching, it can also help to calm your dog in stressful situations.

Capturing Method

Many dogs love a good stretch after getting up or playing, especially if you make playful movements yourself. This is a perfect opportunity to capture the behavior.

1. The moment your dog stretches into a *bow*, mark and reward.
2. When you are confident he will offer the *bow*, say the cue word just before he does it.
3. Encourage your dog to remain in the *bow* position for a longer time by gradually delaying the marker and reward.

Luring Method

1. Show your dog a treat and drop your hand quickly to the floor in front of him between his legs. To follow your hand, he will have to move his nose back and down.
2. If your dog offers anything close to a *bow* to pick up the treat, mark and reward.

Click for Cuteness

The great thing about positive training is that it encourages your dog to show off his creative genius. During "click for cuteness," you allow your dog to be creative and offer any behavior he chooses. If something strikes your fancy, mark and reward it. Click and reward your dog for anything he does that you like, such as rolling on his back while holding a toy, or tilting his head to the side. If he offers the behavior again, mark and reward. Once you are confident that he is just about to offer the behavior, put a name on it and continue to practice for reliability.

You can teach an endless list of tricks with a cardboard box or another safe object that provides lots of interactive options. Place it on the ground. Say nothing. Mark and reward anything your dog does with the object that you find amusing: bumping it with his nose, pushing it, dragging it, opening the lid, climbing in it, or trotting around it!

3. It's okay if your dog stands up or lies down immediately after this, as long as you mark and reward the moment that he is in the *bow* position.
4. To increase the duration of the bow, keep feeding your dog bits of food while he is in the *bow* position.
5. Make the same hand movement to prompt the *bow*, then count to three before you mark and reward.
6. Gradually increase the pause until your dog can hold the *bow* for the count of five.
7. Now make the same hand movement without food in your hand. Mark and offer him a reward from your other hand.
8. Now add the verbal cue "*Bow*" just before you move your hand to cue your dog to go into the *bow*.
9. Practice gradually decreasing your use of the hand signal after saying "*Bow*."
10. Extend the time your dog holds the *bow* position by gradually delaying the marker.

Games

Games are a wonderful way for your dog to expend energy. They also give him a chance to practice valuable life skills. For instance, when playing fetch or any other appropriate game, you can integrate *sits*, *downs*, and hand targets in between periods of play.

Hide-and-Seek/Treasure Hunt

Hide-and-seek lets your dog use his canine instincts to hunt and explore. In this case, he will hunt for a loved one or a favorite treat or toy. It's also a terrific way to encourage him to pay attention to your whereabouts and respond to his name. This game can be played indoors and can also be loads of fun for kids.

1. Have a helper hold your dog and move behind a doorway or a piece of furniture.
2. Once you are out of sight, your helper will tell your dog to find you and release him.
3. As your dog gets better at this game, add to the challenge by hiding farther away in less conspicuous places.

Fetch

The classic game of fetch is not only fun; it also provides great opportunities for your dog to practice cooperation (giving up the toy), earning something that he wants (sit to get another toss), and *coming when called* (as you call your dog back when he picks up the toy). Just because a dog is inclined to chase and grab toys doesn't guarantee that he will bring them back to you and drop them on request. This part of the game usually needs to be taught.

Toys used for fetch should be reserved only for this interaction. Never punish your dog for retrieving the wrong items (such as your shoes). This can discourage him from retrieving. Also, refrain from chasing him when he retrieves something and refuses to bring it back. This will turn the retrieve game into the chase game. Many dogs prefer chasing games, but they won't help him to learn cooperation and compliance.

Capturing Method
1. With your dog on a long leash, toss a toy about 4 feet (1.2 meters) away.
2. Encourage him to run and pick up and bring back the toy.
3. If he doesn't offer to give it back to you, simply remain quiet and try tossing a treat on the floor.
4. Mark and reward with a toss when he drops it.

Agility Fun

In the sport of agility, dogs and handlers are timed as they negotiate a course of obstacles that includes ramps, elevated boards, jumps, see-saws, tire jumps, weave poles, and tunnels. Agility games can be a superb way to actively engage your dog's body and mind. You don't need a serious interest in competitive agility, and you don't need to invest in regulation agility equipment. Small chairs or stools with wooden dowels can be used as jumps, and three to six plungers lined up in a row make great weave poles. Be creative, but don't overlook safety when setting up your agility course. When introducing it to your dog, don't let him overdo it. He needs time and practice to learn to jump and turn safely. Do not to encourage your dog to jump too high or run on slippery flooring.

Jump *On* and *Off*
Teaching your dog to jump *on* and *off* of stable objects on cue is more than an impressive trick. It has many practical uses in daily situations, such as getting in or out of the car, or on or off the furniture.

1. Place a stable object in front of your dog and use your target stick or a hand lure to encourage him to jump *on*.
2. Mark and reward.
3. Now do the same to get him to jump *off*.
4. Repeat.
5. Add a verbal cue for *on* and *off* when you are confident your dog will do it.

PAWS TO CONSIDER

Never practice jumping tricks on a slippery floor.

Jumps should be low enough for your dog to easily leap over without injuring himself. Do not gauge a jump height according to your dog's height. Large or tall dogs are not always adept at jumping. Growing puppies may not have the coordination or strength for jumping exercises.

Jump *Over*

You can teach your dog to jump *over* objects, like a broomstick placed between two chairs, rolled-up blankets, or your leg. This is great exercise and a fun trick, but don't overlook safety.

1. Set up your makeshift hurdle at a low height in a hallway.
2. Stand on one side of the hurdle with your dog. Toss a treat over it and encourage him to go over to the other side to get it.
3. Call him back, reward, and repeat.
4. When your dog learns to *stay* reliably (see Chapter Seven), you can ask him to *sit* on one side of the jump, walk to the other side, and then come to you.

Jump Through a Hoop

Choose a hoop that is large enough for your dog to jump through comfortably. Hula-Hoops without the sound-making beads work well.

1. Rest the hoop on the floor and lean one side against a wall.
2. Mark and reward for any interaction with the hoop (other than chewing on it).
3. Mark and reward when your dog moves toward the hoop and gradually comes closer to stepping through it.

4. You can also toss a treat through the hoop a couple of times to jump-start the behavior.
5. Once your dog is confidently stepping through the hoop while it rests on the floor, gradually raise the height.
6. You can also transfer this skill to teach your dog to jump through your arms, or an agility tire jump.

Tunnel Games

Racing through a tunnel is a fun part of agility, but it can also be taught as a separate trick. You can purchase an agility tunnel made for dogs, which tends to be most durable. Alternatively, you can teach your dog to "tunnel" through a cardboard box with both side flaps taped open, or construct a tunnel by placing a light blanket over a table or two chairs, or even under your bent legs as you sit on the floor.

Capturing Method

1. Put your dog near the tunnel, and mark and reward him or any movement toward it.
2. Gradually reward him only when he moves into the tunnel.
3. Try tossing a piece of food through the tunnel to encourage him.

Targeting Method

1. Teach your dog to target to an object, such as a plastic container or a small placemat.
2. Have a helper hold your dog on one side of the tunnel.
3. Go to the other end and place the target object on the ground directly in front of the tunnel exit (which is collapsed to be as small as possible in the beginning).
4. Encourage your dog to go through the tunnel and touch the target.
5. Mark and reward.

Luring Method

1. Have a helper hold your dog at one end of the tunnel.
2. Go to the other end and reach through to show your dog a high-value treat or toy.
3. Encourage him to follow your lure, and mark and reward when he does.

Weave

For this trick, you need six cones (or plungers) to create a makeshift version of agility weave poles. Always teach your dog to enter the first weave with the pole on his left side in case you decide to move on to competitive agility.

1. Set two cones in a straight line approximately 20 inches (50.8 centimeters) apart.
2. Stand near the first one and wait for your dog to walk past it on his left. Mark and reward.

3. Take a step forward toward the next cone and wait for your dog to step past it to his right. Mark and reward.
4. Repeat.
5. Add another cone to the lineup, and reward him for weaving through them—left, right, left. Gradually add all six cones.

Balance Balls

Teaching your dog to balance on a specially designed, canine balance ball is a terrific way to build muscle strength and coordination.

1. Practice paw targeting with various small objects before introducing a balance ball appropriate for your dog's size.
2. Mark and reward him for any movement toward the ball, or making paw contact.
3. Gradually work toward marking and rewarding him for placing two paws on the ball and then four.
4. You can also teach your dog to target to the ball with just his front or back feet.

Canine Good Citizen

The Canine Good Citizen (CGC) program, administered by the American Kennel Club (AKC), is a noncompetitive test designed to encourage responsible dog ownership. In order to earn this title, dog and handler teams must demonstrate the necessary skills to be safe and mannerly members of the community. The CGC test includes ten exercises to evaluate a dog's temperament and training. To find upcoming tests, visit the AKC website. If your dog qualifies as a CGC, he may be a good candidate for therapy dog work.

Therapy Dogs

The joy that your dog brings to your family and friends can also be shared with people in care facilities including hospitals, nursing homes, and hospice centers. Research has confirmed that contact with dogs has measurable health benefits, such as helping to decrease blood pressure. Dogs are also masters at bringing a smile by simply entering a room and wagging their tails. Mannerly dogs with impulse control who enjoy social interactions with a variety of people may be candidates for therapy dog work. Training programs are offered throughout the country.

Dog Sports

Prior to engaging in any physical activity, be sure to check with your veterinarian to make sure your dog is in good health and up for the challenge. If he is overweight or out of condition, he will need a gradual introduction to an exercise routine.

Frisbee/Disc Dogs

All dog sports are a team effort between dog and human, but none more so than disc sports. Anyone who has watched a disc dog demonstration is surely astounded by the leaps, flips, and lengths to which an enthusiastic canine participant will go to catch the disc in mid-air. For this sport, dogs must be agile, athletic, and highly motivated to catch the disc, and the person must be highly skilled at tossing it predictably for the dog.

Tracking

The dog's superb sense of smell provides them with a vivid interpretation of the world that is quite different than our own. Canine scenting abilities have been put to valuable use over the centuries to hunt, apprehend criminals, and find missing persons. The results have often exceeded the capabilities of even the most modern technologies.

Although every dog possesses a good sense of smell, they vary in their tracking ability. If your dog has a natural talent for following scent trails, you may want to try competitive tracking. You can introduce him to this activity by playing tracking games at home.

Tracking Games at Home

Have someone gently hold your dog as you show him a treat, and then place it on the floor about 10 feet (3 meters) away from him. Go back to your dog and instruct your assistant to let go of his collar when you say *"Find it!"* and send him in search of the treat. Gradually place the treats further away in more complicated places, such as behind the couch. He will have to use his nose to find them.

Swimming

Many dogs love swimming, but do not assume that your dog can swim. Even dogs developed as water retrievers and rescuers benefit from a calm, gradual introduction to swimming. Start with shallow, calm water and be sure not to force your dog to enter. As with children, dogs should always be supervised around water, as even enthusiastic swimmers are susceptible to dangers.

Resources

Finding a Trainer

Andrea Arden Dog Training
www.andreaarden.com
(212) 414-9597

Association of Pet Dog Trainers
(APDT)
101 North Main Street, Suite 610
Greenville, SC 29601
www.APDT.com
(800) PET-DOGS

Animal Behavior Society (ABS)
402 N Park Ave
Bloomington IN 47408
www.animalbehaviorsociety.org
(812)856-5541

Agility

North American Dog Agility
Council (NADAC)
P.O. Box 1206
Colbert, OK 74733
www.nadac.com

United States Dog Agility
Association (USDAA)
PO Box 850955
Richardson, TX 75085-0955
www.usdaa.com
(972) 487-2200

American Kennel Club
http://www.akc.org/events/agility
(919) 816-3725

Rally Obedience
www.apdt.com/rally
(800) PET-DOGS

Clean Run Productions, LLC
17 Industrial Dr.
South Hadley, MA 01075
www.cleanrun.com
(800) 311-6503

Animal Assisted Therapy

Delta Society
875 124th Ave NE #101
Bellevue, WA 98005
www.deltasociety.org
(425) 679-5500

Therapy Dogs International, Inc.
88 Bartley Road
Flanders, NJ 07836
www.tdi-dog.org
(973) 252-9800

Kennel Clubs

American Kennel Club (AKC)
8051 Arco Corporate Drive, Suite 100
Raleigh, NC 27617-3390
www.AKC.org
(919) 233-9796

Canadian Kennel Club (CKC)
200 Ronson Drive, Suite 400
Etobicoke, Ontario
M9W 5Z9
www.ckc.ca
416-675-5511

General Pet Care

The Whole Dog Journal
P.O. Box 5656
Norwalk, CT 06854
www.whole-dog-journal.com
(800) 829-9165

Dog Modeling
www.DogActorsGuild.com

Index

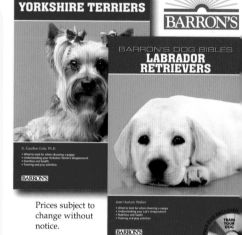
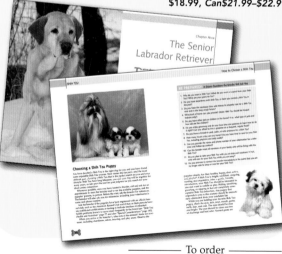